ITALY

ITALY

ITALY

MARTIN HÜRLIMANN

225 PICTURES IN PHOTOGRAVURE

INTRODUCTORY ESSAY

HISTORICAL NOTES

THAMES AND HUDSON · LONDON

Published April 1953

Reprinted October 1953

PRODUCED BY THAMES AND HUDSON LTD LONDON AND ATLANTIS VERLAG ZURICH
PRINTED IN GREAT BRITAIN BY JARROLD AND SONS LTD NORWICH
GRAVURE PLATES PRINTED BY ETS BRAUN ET CIE MULHOUSE

ITALY

———————

FOR generations past Europeans north of the Alps have looked upon Italy as the land of their dreams, a country where more favoured human beings live and thrive beneath a more generous sun. They have come to regard it as the land of noble invention and lofty achievement, a country of churches and palaces overflowing with works of art; an incomparable treasure-house still, despite losses incurred down the centuries through the acquisitions of foreigners for their own enrichment or the endowment of national museums.

Goethe, the world-citizen, regarded his visit to Italy as the turning-point in his life; Dürer returned from Venice "a changed man", convinced that "art must be won anew for the North". Claude Lorrain and Poussin believed that only in the Roman Campagna irradiated by the spirit of antiquity could they find the ideal landscape which was their goal. While in the peaceful Protestant Cemetery by the Pyramid of Cestus lie two of England's best-loved poets, who, drawn to the classical ideal, ended their all-too-brief lives on Italian soil. Western culture as a whole owes an incalculable debt to Italy as a source of inspiration in the arts.

At the instigation of archaeologists and art historians, academies and institutes were founded in Rome and Florence, the scenes of their most fruitful researches, their most rewarding endeavours. The honour of a sojourn at the Villa Medici on the Pincio in Rome has for the past three hundred years been accorded French painters, sculptors and musicians as a means of achieving final mastery in their particular spheres. Italian is the universal language of fine or beautiful music. Indeed, "beautiful" and "Italy" seem to have become synonymous in men's minds.

But our historic ties with Italy range far beyond the aesthetic realm. Many different peoples have traversed the Alps or crossed the oceans to occupy strategic areas of the peninsula; many foreign armies have fought for European hegemony upon Italy's much-disputed soil. Nor must we forget that for close upon twenty centuries countless millions have made the pilgrimage to the burial church of St Peter, which has become the focal point of the Roman Catholic faith.

The early Romans were our instructors and mentors; they founded European history, and the political ideas which underlay their Republic and their Imperial State are inherent in Western civilization and society today. How was it that this people, having recorded one of the greatest achievements in world history, was for a period of some fifteen centuries thereafter unable to control its own territories, allowing them to become the battle-ground of foreign Powers? How is it that Italy, which contributed so much to the culture of Europe, was unable, until barely a hundred years ago, to achieve national unity and independence? Let us try briefly to bring under review the salient features of this country, which has had so full a measure of both good and ill fortune, which presents to the eye and mind such contrasts and anomalies.

*

Geographically, Italy would seem destined for national sovereignty. We are all of us acquainted with that characteristic jackboot which protrudes south-eastwards into the Mediterranean for a distance of some seven hundred miles, with the "football" of Sicily at its toe. Her coastline accounts for more than two-thirds of Italy's boundaries, while to the north she is separated from the continent of Europe by the Alps; these present a further natural barrier, and serve to complete the self-containedness of this area which belongs as much to the Mediterranean as to Europe. Four-fifths of its surface consists of mountains and hilly country, and does not yield sufficient crops to feed its growing population. The Valley of the Po alone constitutes a wide strip of fertile territory running from Piedmont in the West to the Gulf of Venice, while in the extreme south-east—making up the "heel" of the "boot"—lies the wide and open landscape of Apulia. For the rest, the Apennines and their subsidiary ranges run, like a backbone, down the whole length of the peninsula. From the Maritime Alps at the French frontier to Calabria we encounter the same rugged landscape, with more or less bare ridges and foot-hills, long since denuded of their forests, first by the Romans to build their wooden ships, then by the Venetians and the Genoese; from this wholesale and oft-repeated pillage the land has not recovered to this day.

Ethnographically, too, we tend to look upon Italy as essentially a unity; the regional variations seem to us no greater—indeed, rather less—than in other countries. At the mention of an Italian, we picture a person of vivacious, often passionate, temperament, with a melodious voice, and theatrical gestures characterized by an air of self-dramatization—an impression partly derived, no doubt, from his appearance on the operatic stage.

Throughout the length and breadth of Italy we encounter the same type of settlement, close by the big towns of the plain, beside natural harbours and at river-crossings: little townships, clinging to the side of a hill or, preferably, perched upon its summit and spilling down its flanks; a congeries of unpretentious flat-roofed houses dominated by a campanile, by a castle or by those rectangular towers which the ruling houses of the Middle Ages were wont to erect, perpetuating in stone their ancient rivalries.

The provincial towns where the 272 archbishops or bishops of Italy have their sees all developed along similar historical lines. There is the Duomo or cathedral—for the most part Romanesque, sometimes with a projecting Baroque façade—representing the hub of the community; its spacious interior used to serve not only for Divine Service, but also as a meeting-place for those who conducted the affairs of the parish. In the later Middle Ages the citizenry, as it grew more influential, built its own Palazzo della Raggione or Palazzo Comunale, whose secular tower was sometimes made to overtop the campanile of the church. At the same time the ruling houses in the land had elaborate palaces built, and these, too, were ornamented with towers—visual tokens of their ducal, but often also tyrannical power.

It is not alone the monuments of the Middle Ages and of the Renaissance that reflect this communal life; in the old town centre to this day we detect the political pulse of the people. At certain times of the day the Corso, the Piazza del Duomo or the Piazza Comunale swarm with citizens who have gathered there to discuss public or private business, and on occasions the babble of their voices rises to a crescendo.

Another characteristic feature of this land is that, beyond the towns, no peasantry of anything like comparable importance is to be found; nor is there a landed gentry to which members of the rural community might aspire.

As long ago as in Roman times the peasants, who formed the backbone of the Republican armies, surrendered their independence. Were they lucky, they might themselves become towns-people; otherwise, under the crushing burden of debt, they lost all rights in the land they occupied. From these dispossessed and subject people a proletariat of land-workers was recruited. The owner, however, lived in the town, participating far more in urban matters than in the administration of his domains; he tended to look upon a country estate as a place where he could spend periods of relaxation during the summer months.

This state of affairs has never since materially altered, through all the various changes of individual ownership; to this day the soil of Italy is cultivated not primarily by those who own it, but either by an anonymous army of land-workers, as on the large estates of the South, or by small farming-tenants who, as in fertile Tuscany where they retain one half of the produce for themselves, have achieved a certain degree of prosperity. One misses the well-ordered villages and handsome farmsteads of countries north of the Alps.

Italy builds in stone. Mighty cubes of hewn rock carry the towers of town hall and palace, brick walls are fashioned into solid masses and faced with travertine, slabs of white and coloured marble decorate the façades of churches. These solid structures mostly have a sombre hue, in keeping with a rugged landscape exposed to all the winds that blow and the parching midday sun. It is against such a background that the beguiling dreams of the romantic spirit find their realization: those orange and lemon groves that Goethe immortalized, those fountains gushing into marble basins flanked by cypress and myrtle, those pinewoods through whose dark tracery one catches glimpses of shimmering blue water and sails drifting by.

*

That national unity which seems so natural a thing to us today has a background of be-wilderingly diverse historical factors, which prevented a political unification of Italy from the inside until quite recent times. In 500 B.C. *Italia* was the name given to the district of Calabria, while in later centuries it came to embrace the whole area south of Upper Italy; under Augustus it signified most of what we now understand by the name Italy—and at that time, too, the country first came under unified control. Nevertheless, if we are to talk about a Kingdom of Italy during or after the tribal migrations, the extreme South and several other important regions of the present-day Republic must be excluded.

The historian or ethnologist who wishes to trace back the characteristics of the Italian people to any particular race is faced with a singular medley of origins. It was not until well into the Middle Ages that the tribal migrations which affected the Apennine peninsula from prehistoric times onwards, finally came to an end. Long before the Romans built their routes over the passes, the natural barrier of the Alps had not hindered tribes from North, East and West from seeking new habitats far from the fogs and forests of their homelands. So far as it has been possible to ascertain, some of these races crossed the Alps to settle in the plains to the South. Nor did the coasts, for their part, prevent seafaring Mediterranean folk from founding their cities on Italian soil, or, alternatively, from engaging in raids of pillage and plunder. Thus we find Italy, at the time of the first reliable historical records, occupied by a colourful mixture of races: there were the Latins who, having come down from the North—probably from areas around the Central Alps—settled in the district around the Alban hills and, pene-trating thence into the Campagna, became the founder-race of Rome. In the North-west were the Ligurians, in the North-east the Venetians, in the South the Phoenicians and the Greek colonists. Opinions differ as to the exact origins of the Etruscans and their still undeciphered language, though they are believed to have come from somewhere in Asia Minor. These gifted peoples brought with them a highly developed culture; though they came under the political control of Rome, their influence upon contemporary Graeco-Roman civilization was con-siderable. Indeed, Italian achievement down the ensuing centuries owes much to this original infusion of the creative genius of the Etruscans. The last influx of the Celts dates back to the time of the rise of the Roman Republic (about 400 B.C.), when the invaders settled in Upper Italy.

Once Rome had come to rule the entire peninsula, the infiltration of foreign influences came about in a different manner; the thousands of prisoners-of-war, of slaves and mercenaries from all over the Mediterranean area and Northern Europe, upon which the Empire came to depend more and more, in due course demanded rival rights and ultimately fused with the main body of the Italian people.

The sack of Rome by the Visigoths under Alaric in A.D. 410 was the signal for the disintegration of Rome's world-power. It opened the way to a succession of onslaughts from the North by barbarian races, who could no longer be contained. The Visigoths were followed by the Huns; then the Ostrogoths founded their Italian kingdom in Verona and Ravenna, and these were succeeded by the visitations of the Lombards. Even as late as the tenth century, one of the many roving warlike tribes, the Hungarians, were still endangering Upper Italy with their predatory raids. Meanwhile, the Byzantine emperors were making great efforts, with varying degrees of success, to realize their dream of inheriting the mantle of their Roman predecessors and becoming the legitimate heirs to the latters' throne.

As a result of the Frankish King Pippin's donation to the Pope in 754, which marked the founding of the Papal States, and of the crowning of Pippin's son Charles by Leo III on Christmas Day, 800, two new world powers came into being: the Pope, representing the spiritual sovereignty of Christendom, and the Germano-Roman emperor, representing the temporal. Throughout the Middle Ages the fate of Italy was determined by the clashes between these two dominant influences. Neither, it is true, was strong enough to mould the peninsula into a unified political entity comparable, say, with the Sicilian-Apulian dominion of Frederick II some four centuries later.

Gradually the towns, particularly those in Upper Italy, outgrew the tutelage of their bishops, became independent communities with a high degree of self-reliance; they went through phases of oligarchic, and subsequently of monarchic government, and finally won their own say in the country's affairs by virtue of the part they played in trade and commerce. They knew how to thwart every attempt at unification which threatened to infringe their individual liberty. What is more, they carried on feuds one against the other; the bitter struggle between Guelph and Ghibelline—itself a phase in the protracted trial of strength between Emperor and Pope—was but one of many manifestations of this intense local rivalry.

We have sought to provide, in the Notes that accompany the pictures in this volume, some of the more important pieces making up the complicated mosaic that is Italian history in the Middle Ages and after. There reference is made to the far-reaching and often powerful, yet never quite consolidated Papal States; to the leading families which attained to dukedoms, such as the Visconti and Sforzas in Milan, the Gonzagas in Mantua, the Estes in Modena, the Medici in Florence, and the house of Savoy in Savoy and Piedmont; to Mediterranean trade and commerce, which was monopolized by the Republics of Genoa and Venice, once they had ousted their rivals Amalfi and Pisa; to Florence, which became Italy's banking centre; to Milan and the rest of Lombardy, the one-time territory of the race from which it derived its name, whose fate was time and again determined by the confederates who controlled the central crossing of the Alps.

The South had long been a stronghold of the Saracens; in the ninth century they capture the hitherto Byzantine island of Sicily and cross the Straits to the mainland—in 846 they even reach the outskirts of Rome and burn down the basilicas of St Peter and St Paul which lay outside the walls.

In the eleventh century they are followed by the Normans, who found the kingdom of Naples and Sicily, which is to lead an independent existence until the nineteenth century; in 1186 it falls by marriage to the house of Hohenstaufen, against whom the Pope allies himself with Charles of Anjou, and from now on the French play nearly as important a rôle in the destinies of Italy as have the Germans hitherto.

In Sicily, mounting dissatisfaction with this foreign domination leads to the bloody revolt of the Sicilian Vespers (1282); but, in order to rid themselves of the hated Anjou, the Sicilians have to call upon yet another foreigner, this time King Peter of Aragon. In the ensuing struggle for the "Two Sicilies" between French and Spaniards, the latter ultimately gain the upper hand; from 1504 on, there is a resident viceroy in Naples.

Finally, the rise of the Habsburgs leads to the centuries-long conflict which rages on Italian soil between Austria and France: from the capture of Francis I by Charles V at Pavia (1525) to the Battle of Solferino (1859), when Napoleon III, in alliance with the King of Sardinia, defeats the young Emperor Francis Joseph. This decisive event paved the way for the diplomacy of the great liberal statesman Cavour, who reconciled the conflicting interests of the patriot leader Garibaldi, the Papal States and the throne, with the result that the first truly Italian kingdom was born.

This century sees this new nation already so firmly established, that neither the war of 1914–18, nor the change-over from monarchy to republic, nor even the shattering events of the Second World War could undermine it.

*

But long before she actually achieved national sovereignty, Italy was a concept latent within the consciousness of her people. Her politico-military history presents us with but one side of the picture; her achievements in the realm of the arts, offer a very different one.

In Florence, in the year 1265, Dante Alighieri was born. During his restless life, which drew to its close at the court of his friend Guido Novella da Polenta in Ravenna fifty-six years later, and which mirrored the disjointed times in which he lived, he wrote the *Divine Comedy*.

Not only did he thereby give to the Western world its noblest poetical work, but with its appearance, as if by a miracle, the Italian tongue was transformed into the great cultural language that it has remained ever since. At the same time, the legendary figure of Dante served to kindle in the Italian people a growing sense of their mission in the world: a poet became the father of a nation.

Contemporaneously, another Florentine created in Rome, Padua, Florence and Assisi frescoes of singular significance: Giotto di Bodone is the first of a remarkable line of painters, sculptors and architects who, particularly during the *quattrocento*, produced a quite astonishing abundance of great works of art; to one or other of these masters every subsequent art style owes a debt, be it to Raphael or Michelangelo, Piero della Francesca or Leonardo, Masaccio or Mantegna, Donatello or Caravaggio. Italy, which in Rome once transmuted the Spartan virtues into world-history, now revives the genius of Athens.

By the sixteenth century the driving force and creative originality of the Renaissance have already spent themselves; art falls back into the commonplace, the imitative or the mannered. But there is to be yet one more artistic flowering, when Bernini and his contemporaries give visual expression to the pathos of the Counter-Reformation; by merging architecture, the plastic arts and naturalism, and breathing into the slightly theatrical issue an abundance of life, they achieve a unity never before known. They have given us the Roman fountains with their play of light and shade on water and stone; the colonnades of St Peter's Square create a link between the isolated grandeur of Michelangelo's dome and the proud elevations of Pontifex Maximus, while Juvara composes the palace-like structure which is the church of the Superga as a triumphant centre-piece for the Turin landscape.

Then, after a last brief re-kindling in Venice, with Tiepolo and Guardi, the fire is extinguished. Italy's mastery in the visual arts seems over; yet we still encounter in the streets of Florence and Rome the same heads, full of character and poise, as appear in the frescoes of Mantegna and on the reliefs of the Augustan Age—the living face of Italy.

*

The Italian State came to its final realization only after the other European nations had consolidated themselves in the nineteenth and twentieth centuries. Italy did not take part in the rivalry of the German, Austrian, French, English, Spanish and Russian dynasties—a rivalry out of which the great latter-day Powers grew. The political aptitude of the people from which Roman Law evolved and which, from Dante and Machiavelli to Benedetto Croce, has palpably enriched our heritage of political thought, found expression in other ways. The Italian nation's creative contribution to European history did not restrict itself to purely nationalistic aspirations, but took the whole world for its province.

The reality of the community, so simply ordered, with the office of bishop as the shepherd of the parish, forms the solid foundation upon which the nation is built—a nation which first took shape in the language of a Dante, of a Giotto, of a St Francis of Assisi; and the visions of the saints, poets and painters were for this land no less real than victories on the field of battle or the crafty alliances of princes.

The Christian-hellenistic spirit informed the mind of Empire, which was symbolized in Rome—and only in Rome could a true Caesar be crowned. In Rome the Vicar of Christ has his see, and the long line of outstanding personalities who have occupied the Papal throne testify to the pre-eminence of the Italian in his own province, the universal.

*

The pictures in this book are intended to provide an overall impression of Italy, such as might be gained by a leisured traveller who, starting from the Alps, proceeds southwards in a series of zigzags down the peninsula, to end up on the island of Sicily.

Having traversed the Great St Bernard Pass, we follow an imposing military highway into the Aosta Valley; there we meet with French customs and types, just as in the southern Alpine valleys farther east the atmosphere is German, while the Ticino for its part has, under the protection of Swiss federalism, preserved intact its Italianate character. Skirting the Alps, we encounter along the genial shores of the Lakes the first palm trees and cypresses. Up the Valtellina we pass once more through a region of the High Alps to the jagged Dolomites, till, following the shores of Lake Garda, we reach the broad valley of the Po.

Across this fertile plain is strung a chain of towns which have long served as centres of culture: Milan, Vicenza, Pavia, Padua and, set like a jewel in a lagoon of the Adriatic, the fabulous city of Venice, where there are no road vehicles to shatter the age-old quiet, and where in the shadow of the Byzantine splendour of St Mark's the pigeons alone share with the populace the amenities of the world-famous Piazza.

Mantua, Cremona, Parma, Bologna, Ferrara; everywhere we find cathedrals and palaces. Amid isolated relics of antiquity, they have bequeathed to us the urban culture of the Middle Ages and of the Renaissance in countless historic monuments. Ravenna transports us back to the time of the tribal migrations: the tomb of that great barbarian ruler, Theodoric the Ostrogoth, stands as a lasting memorial to his age, while in the churches the Byzantine mosaics gleam as they did fourteen centuries ago.

Crossing the Apennines, we reach the Gulf of Genoa on the west coast, and can follow it down by way of the Levantine Riviera and past the marble buttresses of the Carrara mountains, to Pisa. The sea has since receded from this once important maritime centre; its cathedral, baptistery and leaning tower of gleaming marble now stand apart in the open glade which was to have served the Ghibelline town as a kind of imperial Forum. By way of Lucca, Pistoia, Prato we are led to the enchanting uplands of Tuscany, to Florence, where Lorenzo the Magnificent, a second Pericles, gathered about him the philosophers and artists of a re-awakened antiquity.

On to Siena, and from there we cross the Apennines once more to the Adriatic coast, where we skirt Rimini at the meeting-point of the via Emilia and the via Flaminia. After a visit to Raphael's birthplace, Urbino, we continue through hilly country to Perugia, focal point of the Umbrian school of painting, and on to Assisi, where the nation celebrates its religious re-birth out of the spirit of poverty. Having penetrated the rugged Abruzzi and admired the grandeur of the snow-covered Gran Sasso, we turn westward again through Spoleto, Orvieto and Viterbo and down through the Campagna to the monument-filled capital of the Ancient World.

In the South, too, in the former Kingdom of the Two Sicilies, we traverse Roman roads, pass beneath Roman arches, while in Pompeii we come face to face with an ancient Roman town just as it was when engulfed by lava and ashes in the year A.D. 79.

How different is the imprint of Greece on Italian soil, as we meet it still farther south in the shape of the three temples at Paestum, rising in all their shapeliness and dignity by the Gulf of Salerno. And yet another world opens up when we approach the Adriatic coast once more, and pass into Apulia: hard by the cathedrals and the picturesque harbour towns rise the lonely castles of the Hohenstaufen emperor Frederick II, the only German ruler who still lives on as a legendary figure in the consciousness of the Italian people. Here, too, hinting at cultures of bygone ages, stand the Trulli, prototypes of the cupolas which in the hands of Brunelleschi, Bramante and Michelangelo were to become the pride and triumph of Italian architecture.

Once more across the mountains, the cloud-hung Basilicata of Lucania, into Calabria, and we are approaching our final goal, Sicily. Encompassed on all sides by the waters of the Mediterranean, Sicily has been settled in turn by Greeks, by Phoenicians, by Saracens, by Normans; it has been occupied by Germans, French and Spaniards. Yet it has retained throughout the years its essential national character, the universal character of Italy.

*In addition to Martin Hürlimann's photographs
material for reproduction was supplied by
Doris Bivetti-Gattiker (Plates 220, 221 and 225)
and Anderson of Rome (Plate 223)*

GRAN S. BERNARDO

VALLE DEL GRAN S. BERNARDO

2

AOSTA. CHIOSTRO DI S. ORSO

3

COURMAYEUR

4

MONTE BIANCO (MONT BLANC)

CERVINO (MONT CERVIN, MATTERHORN)   6

VAL D'AOSTA. VILLENEUVE

7

VAL D'AOSTA

8

FORTE DI BARD, VAL D'AOSTA

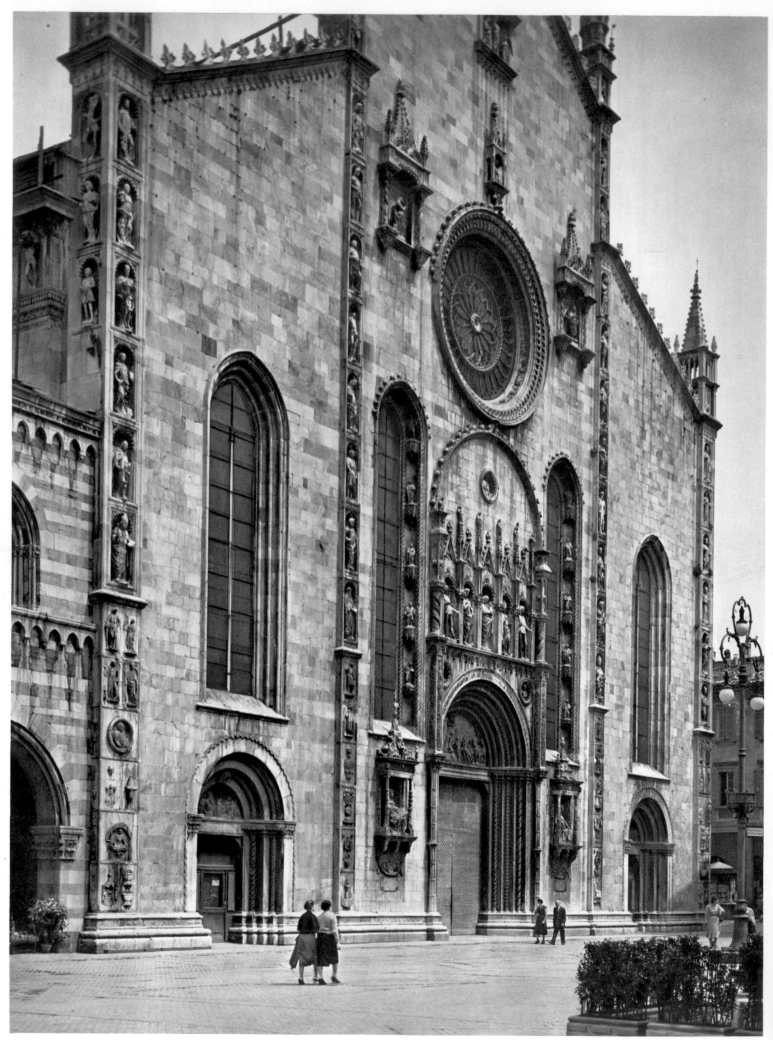

COMO, DUOMO

SUPERGA, TORINO

STRESA, LAGO MAGGIORE

FERIOLO, LAGO MAGGIORE

PALLANZA, LAGO MAGGIORE

14

GANDRIA, LAGO DI LUGANO

VALTELLINA 16

VALTELLINA 17

STELVIO (STILFSERJOCH)   18

PASSO DELLO STELVIO (STILFSERJOCH)   19

ORTLES (ORTLER)

SASSO LUNGO, PASSO DI SELLA (SELLAJOCH)   21

PASSO DI SELLA. DOLOMITI   22

GRUPPO DI SELLA

23

PASSO DI COSTALUNGA (KARERPASS)

LAGO DI CAREZZA (KARERSEE). LATEMAR

TRENTO

LAGO DI TOBLINO

RIVA SUL GARDA

LAGO DI GARDA

SALÒ

SIRMIONE. ROCCA SCALIGERA

FASANO. LAGO DI GARDA

BERGAMO, S. MARIA MAGGIORE

MILANO, CASTELLO SFORZESCO

MILANO. DUOMO

PAVIA, PONTE COPERTO

CERTOSA DI PAVIA

BRESCIA, LOGGIA

VERONA, PORTA DEI BORSARI

39

VERONA, PONTE SCALIGERO

VERONA, PIAZZA DEI SIGNORI

ERONA, PALAZZO DEL COMUNE

VERONA, ARCHE SCALIGERE

VERONA, S. ZENO MAGGIORE

44

VICENZA, LOGGIA DEL CAPITANIO

VICENZA. VILLA ROTONDA

VICENZA, BASILICA

PADOVA, PALAZZO DELLA RAGIONE

48

PADOVA. GATTAMELATA. BASILICA DI S. ANTONIO   49

VENEZIA. PIAZZA S. MARCO

VENEZIA, PALAZZO DUCALE

VENEZIA, PIAZZETTA

VENEZIA, PALAZZO DUCALE

VENEZIA, PONTE DEI SOSPIRI

VENEZIA, PALAZZO VENDRAMIN CALERGI

VENEZIA. CANAL GRANDE, S. MARIA DELLA SALUTE

VENEZIA, CA' D'ORO

VENEZIA, PONTE DI RIALTO

VENEZIA, SUL CANAL GRANDE

VENEZIA. B. COLLEONI

VENEZIA, RIO DEI MENDICANTI

CHIOGGIA

MANTOVA, S. LORENZO

MANTOVA. PALAZZO DUCALE, DUOMO

CREMONA, DUOMO

MODENA, DUOMO

MODENA
68

FIDENZA, CATTEDRALE
69

PARMA, BATTISTERO

BOLOGNA, PIAZZA DEL NETTUNO

BOLOGNA, STRADA MAGGIORE

BOLOGNA

FERRARA, CASTELLO ESTENSE

FERRARA, CATTEDRALE

RAVENNA, CALCHI

RAVENNA, MAUSOLEO DI TEODORICO

RAVENNA, PINETA

RAVENNA, S. VITALE

S. APOLLINARE IN CLASSE (RAVENNA)

APPENNINO EMILIANO

PASSO DELLA FUTA (APPENNINO EMILIO - TOSCANO)

GENOVA

PORTOFINO

S. MARGHERITA LIGURE

RAPALLO

RIVIERA DI LEVANTE

PISA, PIAZZA DEI CAVALIERI

PISA, CAMPANILE

PISA, BATTISTERO

PISA, PERGAMO DEL DUOMO

LUCCA, BASILICA S. FREDIANO

LUCCA, DUOMO

PISTOIA, OSPEDALE DEL CEPPO

PISTOIA, OSPEDALE DEL CEPPO

PRATO. DUOMO, PERGAMO DEL SACRO CINGOLO

FIRENZE

FIRENZE, PONTE VECCHIO

FIRENZE, CAMPANILE

FIRENZE, PALAZZO PITTI

FIRENZE, BARGELLO

FIRENZE, PIAZZA DELLA SIGNORIA

FIRENZE, PIAZZA S. SPIRITO

FIRENZE, S. MARIA NOVELLA, CHIOSTRO VERDE

FIRENZE, GIARDINO DI BOBOLI

S. GIMIGNANO

PAESAGGIO TOSCANO (S. GIMIGNANO)

VAL D'ARNO

AREZZO, S. MARIA DELLE PIEVE

SIENA, PALAZZO PUBBLICO

SIENA, DUOMO

APPENNINO

UMBERTIDE

SARSINA

RIMINI, ARCO D'AUGUSTO

116

RIMINI, PONTE D'AUGUSTO

117

ANCONA, ARCO DI TRAIANO

LORETO

PAESAGGIO DELLE MARCHE

FOSSOMBRONE

URBINO

DINTORNI DI URBINO

VAL DEL BURANO

CANTIANO

PERUGIA, FONTANA MAGGIORE

PERUGIA

S. MARIA DEGLI ANGELI

ASSISI, BASILICA S. FRANCESCO

ASSISI, CONVENTO S. FRANCESCO

131

ASSISI, S. FRANCESCO, CHIESA SUPERIORE

132

ASSISI, TEMPIO DI MINERVA

133

GRAN SASSO

134

ANTRODOCO (ABRUZZI)

135

L'AQUILA, CASTELLO. GRAN SASSO

136

L'AQUILA, S. MARIA DI COLLEMAGGIO

137

L'AQUILA, S. BERNARDINO

LUGNANO IN TEVERINA

AMELIA

SPOLETO, PONTE DELLE TORRI

ORVIETO.

ORVIETO, DUOMO

143

VITERBO, VIA S. PELLEGRINO

VITERBO, PALAZZO PAPALE

LAGO DI BOLSENA

RONCIGLIONE

TARQUINIA

148

GROSSETO

149

ROMA, PORTA S. SEBASTIANO

ROMA, FORUM ROMANUM

ROMA, ISOLA TIBERINA

ROMA, GIANICOLO

153

ROMA. PONTE E CASTEL S. ANGELO

154

ROMA, PIAZZA DI SPAGNA

ROMA, FONTANA DEI FIUMI

ROMA, FONTANA DI TREVI

ROMA, S. CLEMENTE

ROMA. CAMPIDOGLIO E S. MARIA D'ARACOELI

159

ROMA, S. GIOVANNI IN LATERANO

160

ROMA, PIAZZA S. PIETRO

ROMA, PIAZZA S. PIETRO

ROMA, TEMPIO DI VESTA E TEMPIO DELLA FORTUNA VIRILE

VIA APPIA

PALESTRINA

TIVOLI

TIVOLI, VILLA D'ESTE

CASTEL GANDOLFO. CAMPAGNA ROMANA

FRASCATI, VILLA ALDOBRANDINI

ITRI   170

CASERTA, PALAZZO REALE

IL VOLTURNO A CAPUA

S. MARIA CAPUA VETERE, ANFITEATRO

TROIA, CATTEDRALE

MONTESARCHIO 175

BENEVENTO, CHIOSTRO 176

BENEVENTO, ARCO DI TRAIANO

POMPEI, VIA DEI SEPOLCRI

POMPEI, FORO   179

POMPEI, FORO E BASILICA   180

POMPEI, TEMPIO D'APOLLO

POMPEI, CASA DEL FAUNO

POMPEI, GIARDINO DI LOREIUS TIBURTINUS

NAPOLI, CASTEL NUOVO

NAPOLI

COSTIERA SORRENTINA E CAPRI

SORRENTO

POSITANO

POSITANO

AMALFI

MINORI

COSTIERA AMALFITANA

ATRANI

GOLFO DI SALERNO

PAESTUM. TEMPIO DI NETTUNO E BASILICA

PAESTUM, TEMPIO DI CERERE

PAESTUM, BASILICA

LUCERA, CASTELLO

CAPITANATA (PUGLIA)

CASTEL DEL MONTE

TRANI, CATTEDRALE

MOLFETTA

BARI, S. GREGORIO E S. NICOLA

BARI, CASTELLO   204

BRINDISI, S. GIOVANNI AL SEPOLCRO   205

MURGIA DEI TRULLI (PUGLIA)

TRULLO

ALBEROBELLO

LOCOROTONDO

TARANTO, CASTELLO

TARANTO, BORGO

LAGONEGRO, APPENNINO LUCANO

APPENNINO LUCANO 213

MORANO CALABRO 214

TAORMINA

TAORMINA

SIRACUSA, TEATRO GRECO

217

SIRACUSA, GROTTA DEI CORDARI

218

SIRACUSA. DUOMO

SELINUNTE

AGRIGENTO

PALERMO

MONREALE, DUOMO

223

PALERMO, DUOMO

SEGESTA

HISTORICAL NOTES

1 GREAT ST BERNARD, Hospice. The pass, over 8,000 feet high, which connects the Aosta Valley with the Valais, was used already by the Romans as one of the most important links between Italy and the countries north of the Alps. In the vicinity of the lake there are still remains of Roman buildings, among them a temple dedicated to Jupiter Penninus. Charlemagne, the Emperor Henry IV on the way to Canossa, Frederick Barbarossa, Napoleon—all led considerable armies south across the pass at various times. Our plate shows the view towards Italy from the hospice which stands on Swiss soil.

2 Following the GREAT ST BERNARD VALLEY the southward-bound traveller soon leaves behind the characteristic Alpine scenery. Beyond the village of Gignod this more open country leads down into the Aosta Valley.

3 AOSTA. The chief town of the province, founded by the Romans under the name of *Augusta Praetoria* in 25 B.C. Birthplace of the great churchman Anselm of Canterbury (1033–1109), it contains prized mediaeval buildings, besides Roman monuments. The Romanesque cloisters of the Collegiata of S. Orso date from the twelfth century.

4 COURMAYEUR, 4,016 feet, the oldest health resort and sports centre in the Italian Alps, lies at the foot of the Mont Blanc massif.

5 View from Courmayeur towards Mont Blanc, the highest mountain in Europe (15,782 feet), with its subsidiary peaks and glaciers.

6 A mighty pyramid of gneiss, 14,782 feet high, the famous Matterhorn (Ital. Monte Cervino), towers above Breuil (Ital. Cervinia).

7–9 Through the AOSTA VALLEY runs the Dora Baltea, which derives from the snows of Mont Blanc; this is a French-speaking zone and enjoys a certain degree of autonomy.

7 The little church of Villeneuve.

8 The castles on the hill-tops recall the fact that this valley was of strategic importance also in the Middle Ages.

9 In the south-east the valley is virtually sealed off by the fortress of Bard, which dominates the village of like name. This fortress was built in the fifteenth century by the House of Savoy, and replaced a castle belonging to the Counts of Bard dating from the eleventh century. In 1800 Napoleon broke through the Austrian-Piedmontese troops who were defending the valley, and razed the fortress; it was rebuilt in 1830 (by King Charles Albert).

10 The episcopal see of COMO (Latin *Comum*), subject since 1335 to Milan, was known already in the early Middle Ages as the home of leading architects and sculptors. The Cathedral, rebuilt in marble some time after 1396, was given its ornamental façade by the brothers Rodari between 1463 and 1486. The projecting niches on either side of the central porch contain the statues of Como's two great sons of Roman times, the Elder and Younger Pliny.

11 On a rise at the eastern fringe of the large industrial city of TURIN stands the Basilica of the SUPERGA, built in 1717–31 by Juvara. With its 250-feet-high dome, it is one of the most imposing examples of Baroque architecture. Victor Amadeus II of Savoy erected this church to commemorate the liberation of Turin, which had been besieged by the French in 1706. Buried in the crypt are the Kings of Sardinia and the Princes of Savoy, to whose house Turin (the Roman *Augusta Taurinorum*) belonged since the thirteenth century. Focus of the Risorgimento in the nineteenth century, Turin was for five years from 1861 the first capital of the newly united Kingdom of Italy.

12–14 The LAGO MAGGIORE (called *Lacus Verbanus* by the Romans) is 40 miles long, and is the second largest lake in Upper Italy. The north end is situated in the Swiss canton of Ticino, and the river of that name flows through the lake. Along the sheltered western shore between Pallanza and Stresa is a profusion of hotels and villas amid luxuriant vegetation.

12 Lakeside view from the health resort of Stresa, looking towards the two Borromee islands. On the nearer of the two, the Isola Bella, can be seen the terraced gardens laid out by Count Vitaliano Borromeo between 1650 and 1671.

13 The fishing village of Feriolo, also on the western shore.

14 Palm-trees and oleanders at Pallanza.

15 The eastern, Italian end of the Lake of Lugano, seen from the Swiss frontier town of Gandria.

16–17 The Valtellina, 75-mile-long valley of the Adda, which runs between the south Rhaetian and the Bergamo Alps, and debouches into the Lake of Como. Subject to Milan, this strategically important valley, famed for its vineyards, was a province of the Swiss canton of Graubünden from 1512 to 1797; Napoleon incorporated it into the Cisalpine Republic; after the Treaty of Villafranca in 1859, Austria ceded it to Italy.

18–20 THE STELVIO PASS, 9,042 feet high, close to the Swiss frontier, connects the Adda and Adige valleys, running between the "Peak of Three Languages" and Monte Scorluzzo. The last part of the Alpine road, built in 1820–5, mounts steeply in a series of hairpin bends from the Trafoi valley (Plate 19). From the top of the Pass one obtains fine views, northwards into Switzerland (Plate 18), where the Umbrail road leads into the Münsterthal (the Bormio Pass), and, eastwards, of the Ortles Range (Plate 20), whose summit is 12,802 feet high.

21–23 THE SELLA RANGE belongs to the mountain region known as the Dolomites. These jagged mountains rise up like columns or bastions from green uplands of marl and sandstone, and are the most beautiful region of the "Chalk Alps". In the west, erosion has resulted in steep and narrow ridges and pinnacles; in the east, in plateau-like limestone masses, whose stratified walls are broken away at varying levels. On the west side of the Sella Pass is the Langkofel, 10,426 feet (Plate 21, beyond the Pass Hotel), and on the east side is the Sella massif, 10,341 feet (Plate 23).

24–25 The PASSO DI COSTALUNGA (5,768 feet) runs, like most of the Dolomite roads, along one of the many saddles of marl and sandstone which intersect the chalk areas of this district. To the north (Plate 24) lies the Rosengarten Group, to the south (Plate 25), as one approaches the Pass from the west, one obtains a fine view of the peaks of the Latemar Range rising (to 9,337 feet) above the waters of the Lago di Carezza (5,020 feet).

26 TRENT, the capital of the Trentino, had its period of glory as a prince-bishopric at the time of the Council of Trent (1545–7, 1552, 1562–3). In 1814 it was Austrian, but became Italian in 1918. In the middle of the Piazza Cesare Battisti rises the Neptune Fountain, erected in 1769. On the left is the Cathedral, the building of which, by Adamo d'Arogno, was begun soon after 1200 and finished in 1515. The Council met here and reached decisions of grave consequence not only for the Church but for the history of the West, leading to the Counter-Reformation.

27 The LAGO DI TOBLINO, which lies between Trent and Lake Garda, with the castle of the Counts of Wolkenstein.

28–32 LAKE GARDA, the largest of the Italian Lakes (216 feet above sea-level, 143 square miles in area) was known until the early Middle Ages by its Roman name of *Benacus*.
"Fluctibus et fremitu resonans Benace marino: the first Latin verse whose meaning stands vividly before me, and which is as true today, at the moment when the wind grows ever stronger and throws ever bigger waves against the shores of the lake, as it was many centuries ago. So much has changed, but the wind still storms across the lake, the sight of which is still ennobled by a line of Virgil" (Goethe).

28 Riva, the harbour town at the north end of the lake.

29 View from Riva to the fiord-like northern arm of the lake.

30 Salò, sheltered on the north side by Monte San Bartolommeo, lies in a bay on the western shore, where the Alps abut on the Lombard Plain.

31 Sirmione, on the long narrow peninsula jutting out at the south end of Lake Garda, with the Rocca Scaligera, the fortress of the powerful Veronese family of Scaliger, built in about 1250. The place, which was important in Roman times as a station on the Via Gallica, was celebrated by Catullus.

32 Fasano: the grounds of one of the summer residences of the aristocratic Venetians in the seventeenth and eighteenth centuries (now an hotel) on the Riviera of Lake Garda, where lemon-trees and cedars, olives and laurels flourish.

33 BERGAMO, at the foot of the Bergamesque Alps, can be traced back to a Celtic settlement. The free commune became Venetian in 1428, and was Austrian from 1814 till 1866. In the upper town, which rises 394 feet above the newer quarter in the plains, the building of the Basilica Santa Maria Maggiore was begun in 1137. The porch, with columns supported by lions, is the work of Giovanni da Campione (1353). The Condottiere Bartolommeo Colleoni had a chapel added to the building, the Capella Colleoni with the family tombs, the work of Giovanni Antonio Omodeo. The façade, with busts of Caesar and Trajan and heads of Augustus and Hadrian introduced in medallions, illustrates (according to Jacob Burckhardt) "the idolization of antiquity of those days". It is "a graceful composition of black, white and red marble, with a variety of sculptures partly taken from the interior, and of the finest ornamental arabesques", and constitutes "one of the most colourful imaginative creations of the fifteenth century".

34-35 MILAN owes her development as the leading industrial and mercantile city of Italy to her position in the middle of the fertile valley of the Po, where the great pass-routes over the Swiss Alps debouch. The *Mediolanum* of ancient times was the chief city of the Celtic Insubres, and became Roman in 222 B.C. In the fourth century, under its great bishop Ambrosius, it was the hub of the Western Church. This powerful city-state was one of the chief supports of the Popes in their struggle against the Roman-German Emperors. In 1512 the reigning Dukes of the later Middle Ages acknowledged the protectorate of the Confederation. Later, Milan came into Spanish and Austrian hands, until in the nineteenth century she was finally able to take a leading place in a newly united Italy.

34 In the courtyard of the Castello Sforzesco, the mighty citadel which Francesco Sforza had built from 1450 onwards on the ruins of the castle of the Visconti. Under Lodovico il Moro, Leonardo and Bramante worked together on this building. The loggia on the right of the picture is ascribed to the latter.

35 In the wide Piazza del Duomo, the central point of the city, is the Cathedral of the Archbishop of Milan. This, the largest Gothic monument in Italy, was built from 1386 onwards by Campionese, and by German, French and Lombardic masters. The façade, begun in 1616, was only finished between 1805 and 1813. In his *Cicerone*, Burckhardt has the following to say of this building: "The Cathedral of Milan is an instructive example, if one wishes to learn to distinguish between an artistic and a fanciful impression. The latter, which one wishes to preserve unimpaired, is in this case overwhelming: a transparent marble mountain, hewn from the quarries of Ornavasso and Gandoglia, resplendent by day and fabulous by moonlight . . . a whole, which cannot be matched elsewhere in the world. But he who seeks permanent worth in its forms, and knows *which* designs remained unrealized while with gigantic resources Milan Cathedral was being finished, will not be able to contemplate this building without grief." And Stendhal speaks of "This brilliant architecture [which] is Gothic minus the idea of death."

36 PAVIA. The Roman *Ticinum*, called Papia by the Lombards, was from 572 till 774 the capital of the Lombard Kingdom and the coronation city of the Regnum Italicum. In the possession of the Visconti from 1364 onwards, it shared the fortunes of Milan and Lombardy. Jurisprudence was already cultivated in Pavia in the tenth and eleventh centuries, long before the foundation of the University proper in 1361. The roofed bridge (Ponte Coperto) over the Ticino was built in 1352-4 on the remains of the Roman building, receiving its roof carried on granite columns in 1583. During the Second World War the bridge was damaged, since when it has been newly built in a slightly different design (photo 1952).

37 CERTOSA DI PAVIA. The Carthusian monastery lying between Pavia and Milan was founded in 1396 by Giangaleazzo Visconti. The church, begun in the Gothic style, has since 1491 been given its existing façade, designed by G. A. Amadeo in variegated marbles, with a portal by Benedetto Briosco (1501). Burckhardt describes it as "the first choice specimen

of ornamental architecture of Italy and of the world"; the most noteworthy example of the Lombard early Renaissance.

38 In the eleventh century BRESCIA became a free commune; later it came into the hands of various noble families, Venetian from 1426 to 1797, and Austrian till 1859. To the building of the so-called Loggia (Palazzo del Comune), the most significant Renaissance building in the town, numerous north Italian artists contributed, among others Tommaso Fromentone, who designed the lower storey, and Jacopo Sansovino, who was responsible for the upper storey: the fenestration derives from Palladio.

39–44 VERONA, at first an Etruscan, then a Gaulish city, became a Roman colony in 89 B.C., and attained, thanks to her strong strategic position at the point of issue of the Adige valley into the Padine Plain, and on the route to the Brenner, a brilliant flowering under the Lombards, and, in the thirteenth and fourteenth centuries, under the rule of the Scaligers. From 1405 till 1796 it belonged to Venice.

39 The double gate called the Porta dei Borsari, is, with the Amphitheatre, among the noteworthy monuments in the town dating from Roman times.

40 The Ponte Scaligero over the Adige, built in the fourteenth century on Roman remains, and fortified. It was almost completely destroyed in 1945, but has since been rebuilt (photo 1952).

41 In the middle of the Piazza dei Signori is the Dante Monument. After his banishment from Florence in 1303 the poet found refuge in Verona at the court of the Scaligers who were Ghibelline sympathizers. On the left is the Loggia del Consiglio (1476–93), the old town hall, designed by the early Renaissance master Fra Giocondo of Verona.

42 Work on the Palazzo del Comune or Palazzo della Ragione was started in 1193; in the courtyard there is a beautiful Gothic external staircase.

43 The Tombs of the Scaligers (Arche Scaligere), beside the Romanesque church of Sta Maria Antica. The tombs, surrounded by a wrought-iron screen of

the fourteenth century, belong to members of the family of della Scala, who ruled in Verona from 1260 till 1387. According to Burckhardt they are "as remarkable from the point of view of cultural history as in point of art. Outside the church, built rather with a politico-monumental purpose than a religious one, by the ruling family of Verona in their own lifetimes, they are the first examples of those entirely secular equestrian statues which were later set up by the Venetians as a political reward for their generals. Here the equestrian statues, still less than life-size, are situated on the apex of each monument." In the foreground, the tomb of Mastino II, completed before 1351, and behind it, that of Cansignorio, finished in 1374 by Bonino da Campione.

44 Eleventh-century bronze reliefs with scenes from the Old and New Testaments on the left-hand leaf of the door of S. Zeno Maggiore, one of the major Romanesque ecclesiastical monuments in northern Italy.

45–47 VICENZA, a Ligurian settlement, Roman after 177 B.C., ruled over by the Scaligers from 1311, then by the Visconti, submitted to the Venetian Republic in 1404. She is renowned for the buildings of the great architect Andrea Palladio (1508 or 1518–80) which served as prototypes for classical design all over Europe, but especially in eighteenth-century England. "The greatest difficulty with which [Palladio], like all modern architects, had to contend, was the problem of adapting column arrangements to secular buildings: there is always a contradiction in the combination of columns and walls. But see how he has contrived the relationship, how he has imposed it through his art, and how he makes us forget that he is merely persuading us!" (Goethe).

45 The Loggia del Capitanio, built by Palladio in 1571.

46 The Villa Rotonda, begun by Palladio in 1550 and finished by Scamozzi, is the most famous of the mansions erected by the former in the neighbourhood of Vicenza, Padua, etc. "Today", wrote Goethe, "I visited the magnificent house called the Rotonda, lying on a pleasant height half an hour from the town. There is great variety in the way the main mass moves in relation to the projecting porticoes as the beholder walks round it. . . . And just as the building

can be seen in all its beauty from every vantage point, so also is the view obtained from it of the pleasantest. One sees the Bacchiglione where it flows, carrying ships from Verona down towards the Brenta; one can see, further, the broad possessions which the Marchese Capra wished to retain undivided in family ownership."

47 The so-called Basilica, one of the earliest of Palladio's works, begun in 1549, but finished only in 1614, encases the Gothic Palazzo della Ragione; beside it, the Torre di Piazza, dating from the twelfth century.

48-49 PADUA, the *Patavium* of the Romans, became a free city in the twelfth century, but was subject to Venice from 1406 till 1797. Its world-famous University was founded in the thirteenth century, and became the leading centre for fostering the study of Jurisprudence.

48 The Palazzo della Ragione was built between 1172 and 1219. The loggias were added to the vast vaulted "Salone" in 1306.

49 Il Santo, the Basilica of S. Antonio, erected 1232-1307 over the tomb of St Antony of Padua (1195-1231). Gothic in its main features, such as the Oriental domes, the building owes much to St Mark's in Venice. Outside, on a lofty pedestal, stands the equestrian statue of Gattamelata, executed by Donatello in 1563 in honour of the condottiere, which was commissioned by the Venetian Republic.

50-62 VENICE arose in the fifth century as the coastal dwellers fled to the islands of the lagoon before the onslaught of the Huns. In 697 the island communities united as the Venetian maritime league under a Doge. The Crusades and the successful wars against the Genoese endowed the Republic with great wealth. As mistress of the Mediterranean, Venice became the most brilliant commercial city in the world: the opulence of her buildings which, as a result of her isolation from the mainland she has retained almost undamaged since the late Middle Ages, mirrors the unprecedented riches of the aristocratic State of the Doges and her close connexions with the Orient, especially with Byzantium. The Peace of Campoformio in 1797 at last sealed the fate of the independent Republic.

50 St Mark's Square, 576 feet by 269 feet, is surrounded by palace façades and bounded at its eastern end by the front of St Mark's. It has the character of an enormous festal hall—Napoleon judged it "the finest salon in the world". Here the great Corpus Christi processions took place and the gorgeous secular fêtes, at which the proud maritime Republic commemorated her victories; or she would celebrate the symbolic "marriage with the sea" at an international fair held before and after Ascension Day, when she would make manifest her opulence and her political ascendency. The pigeons are fed twice a day at the municipal expense, as in the days of the Republic. The Basilica di San Marco was built as the sepulchral church of the city's patron-saint, whose bones were brought to Venice from Alexandria in 829. The building, with its five domes in Byzantine style and an orientally enriched façade, has remained unaltered since the eleventh century. The mighty Campanile, 325 feet high, was built in 900, rebuilt in the fourteenth and sixteenth centuries, and again reconstructed after it had collapsed in 1902.

51 The main entrance to the Doge's Palace, the so-called Porta della Carta, erected in 1438-42 by Giovanni and Bartolomeo Bon. It displays the insignia of the Republic's greatness: a Doge is doing homage to the Lion of St Mark; above St Mark at the top of the tympanum, Justice is enthroned; on left and right are statues of the cardinal virtues.

52 The Piazzetta, the oblong Square joining the Piazza San Marco to the Molo, with a view across the Lagoon towards the island of San Giorgio Maggiore. The church of that name, a tenth-century foundation, was rebuilt by Palladio in 1565-80 and finished in accordance with his plans by Scamozzi in 1610. The Campanile is modelled on that of St Mark (1791). On the left is the west front of the Doge's Palace, on the right the column with the Lion of St Mark.

53 A view of the Doge's Palace, showing also the two columns, monoliths which came from Constantinople or Syria; one carries a bronze lion, the other a statue of St Theodore (the original patron-saint of Venice). In the left foreground can be seen Jacopo Sansovino's masterpiece, the Libreria Vecchia di San Marco (1536-54, finished by Scamozzi, 1582-8). The

Doge's Palace arose in 1309–1404; between 1424 and 1442 the west front facing the Piazzetta was built, and after 1483 the southernmost section of the east front (see Plate 54). This, being in Renaissance style, is sharply distinguished from the other parts. "This wonderful building is now in part a derivation from, and in part a prototype of an important style of palace-architecture, which flourished in Venice in the fourteenth and first half of the fifteenth centuries. It differs from the other Italian (Florentine or Sienese) examples in that it does not derive from the strong family fortresses which served as a hub and refuge for contending political parties. Rather is it peaceful wealth which here turns its serene countenance most willingly upon the Grand Canal. . . . But in the upper storeys, which in the Byzantine epoch had had only very high arched windows on columns, the Gothic style now expresses a daring elaboration of motif: for, above and between the pointed arches there are likewise quatre-foil openings, which are virtually part of the fenestra-tion. In the middle storey a row of such windows is crowded together to form a grand loggia, contrasting excellently with the single-light windows above and below. If one remarks, further, the adornment of the corners with twisted columns, of the wall-surfaces with coloured stonework, of the windows with ogival arches, and of the skyline with Moorish pinnacles, the total impression is one of gaiety and elegance." (Burckhardt: *Cicerone*.)

54 The Bridge of Sighs, built about 1600 by Antonio Contino, connects the Doge's Palace with the Prigioni, the city prison.

55 The Grand Canal, the principal artery of the Lagoon City, is lined on both sides with long rows of luxurious palaces, Gothic and early Renaissance. The Palazzo Vendramini Calergi, formerly Loredan, was designed by Mauro Coducci and brought to completion by the Lombardi (as the Solari family of master-builders were called, after their place of origin) in 1504–9. Here, on February 3rd, 1883, Wagner died. Venice had already made a deep impression on him while he was working at *Tristan* in 1858–9.

56 View from the Ponte dell'Accademia, to the left the Gothic Palazzo Cavalli-Franchetti, dating from the fifteenth century; in the background the dome of Sta Maria della Salute, built by Longhena to commemorate the plague of 1630.

57 The Cà d'Oro on the Grand Canal, a veritable jewel-case of the Gothic, was built in 1422–40 by Lombard architects under the direction of Matteo Raverti, and Venetian masons under Giovanni and Bartolomeo Bon. The gilding of the façade (to which it owes its name) has now disappeared.

58 The Rialto Bridge crosses the Grand Canal at its narrowest point with a marble arch of 91 feet span. It was built in 1588–92 by Antonio da Ponte.

59 On the Grand Canal, near the Fóndaco dei Tedeschi, where the German merchants had their warehouse from the twelfth century onwards.

60 Verrocchio's equestrian monument to Bartolommeo Colleoni (1400–75), leader of mercenaries and patron of art, made between 1481 and 1488. It, and Dona-tello's Gattamelata (Plate 49), are the two finest representations of a condottiere, the personification of the Italian Renaissance hero. Angered by the Senate, who had commissioned the work, Verrocchio had struck off the horse's head and legs; he had to be summoned a second time to Venice to finish his work. In his will (he died in 1488) he entrusted the casting of it to Lorenzo di Credi; the Council of Ten gave Leopardi priority, and he cast the statue in 1496 and erected the marble pedestal.

61–62 The Rio dei Mendicanti opposite the Colleoni memo-rial and (Plate 62) one of the countless smaller canals, which wind between the hundred or so islands of the city. These waterways, most of which are little more than 15 feet wide, are chiefly used for the transport of goods: pedestrians, on the other hand, use the narrow alley called "calli" or "callette". Typical of the Vene-tian houses are the curiously shaped chimneys, also the balconies on which the women like to sit, not only in the evenings but all day long in the glaring sun, to give their hair that red-gold glow to which the painters of the Venetian school have brought renown.

63 CHIOGGIA, in close political association with Venice since the early Middle Ages, spreads over two principal and many smaller neighbouring islands near a Roman

canal, at the southern end of the Lagoon. The town is among the most important fishery centres of Italy, and preserves its popular and picturesque character, at which Goldoni marvelled when he stopped at Chioggia repeatedly and wrote his comedy *Le Baruffe Chiozzote*.

64-65 In MANTUA, one of the north Italian city-states, the house of Gonzaga ruled from 1328 to 1627. Their court, which favoured the arts, was one of the most brilliant of the Renaissance. Among those who worked here were that universal artist, Leon Battista Alberti; the great painter, Mantegna, and later, Castiglione, author of *Il Corteggiano*, and Giulio Romano. In Baroque times, too, music and drama flourished, as under Monteverdi, who was in the service of the Duke from 1590 till 1613 and produced here, among other works, his *Orfeo*. Dante, who related the legendary foundation of Mantua in his *Divine Comedy* (Inferno, XX, 57 et seq.), brought together in a famous encounter in the next world, two poets, Virgil and Sordello, both born in Mantua (Purg., VI, 58 et seq.).

64 The Rotonda di San Lorenzo, a round church on the Piazza delle Erbe, near the Palazzo della Ragione (on the left), was erected about the year 1000 on the ruins of a Roman temple.

65 At the north-west end of the Piazza Sordello is the Cathedral of St Peter. Erected by Giulio Romano and G. B. Covo on the remains of an earlier building which was destroyed by fire in the year 1545, the original Romanesque bell-tower still stands; the Baroque façade was added in 1756. In the foreground is the entrance to the Palazzo Ducale, the castle of the Gonzaga.

66 CREMONA, Roman from 222 onwards, reached her apogee as a free city in the thirteenth century. From 1334 onwards she was ruled by the Milanese Visconti. The widespread fame of the city rests upon her violin workshops, in which Amati, Stradivarius and Guarneri worked during the seventeenth and eighteenth centuries. The façade of the Cathedral, a Romanesque basilica, belongs to later periods: in the fourteenth century Giovanni di Balduccio da Pisa added the projecting portico with figure-decoration on the loggia to the part erected by Giacomo Perrata da Como in 1273. In 1491 Alberto da Carrara began the rebuilding of the side loggias, and in 1501 Pietro da Rho added the pediment with the four statues of the city's patron-saints.

67-68 MODENA, an Etruscan foundation, was in the possession of the Este family from 1288 till 1796, and was from 1598 onwards a ducal seat.

67 The Cathedral, begun in 1099, consecrated in 1184 by Lanfranco, was ornamented by Campionese masters up to the fourteenth century. The west portal, with its reliefs, derives from Wiligelmus (twelfth century).

68 In the southern façade of the Cathedral is the Porta Regia by Anselmo da Campione (1175-1231) and the exterior pulpit by Jacopo da Ferrara (1501). On the right, the Palazzo Comunale, built in 1194, rebuilt in 1624 with a clock-tower; the statue of the Virgin was placed here in 1805.

69 FIDENZA, the Roman *Fidentia*, became known as Borgo San Donnino in the ninth century, but reverted to an adaptation of its ancient Roman name in 1927. The Cathedral, begun in the Romanesque style in 1207, has an elaborate west doorway, which is believed to be the last work of Benedetto Antelami, the most famous Lombard sculptor of this period.

70 PARMA, a Roman colony dating from 183 B.C., was for a time in the Middle Ages an independent city, and came under Papal rule in 1511. In 1545 it became the seat of a Farnese duchy. The red marble Baptistery, which forms an irregular octagon, was built between 1196 and 1260: the balustrade and the turrets were added in 1302-7. On the left, in the foreground, the lion portal of the somewhat earlier Cathedral.

71-73 BOLOGNA, the *Felsina* of the Etruscans and *Bononia* of the Romans, played a leading part in the league of the Lombardic cities in the Middle Ages. The University, founded in 1119, at which Dante and Petrarch (among others) studied, was especially renowned for its jurists. Hence Bologna was known as "la dotta", the learned, but also as "la grassa", the fat, being, as the centre of a rich agricultural district, renowned for her cooking. From 1506 till 1860 she mostly belonged to the Papal States.

71 On the Piazza del Nettuno stands the Fountain of Neptune, designed by Tommaso Laureti, and with bronzes by Giovanni da Bologna, called Giambologna (1566). Behind it is the Palazzo Comunale, with its entrance adorned with a statue by Mengati (1580) of the Bolognese Pope Gregory XIII, who reformed the calendar.

72 Strada Maggiore (Via Mazzini), one of the streets which radiate from the centre of the city, which is laid out on a concentric plan. The characteristic arcades, together with the colour of the many Gothic brick buildings, lend this ancient centre of Western culture its unique character.

73 The Torre degli Asinelli, 320 feet high, and the unfinished Torre dei Garisendi, 156 feet high, both leaning, are survivors of the 200 or so family towers of the mediaeval town. The inclination of the "Garisenda" is already mentioned by Dante.

74-75 FERRARA had her great period under the Este, who ruled the town from 1208 till 1598. At their brilliant court, well-disposed to humanistic studies, to painting and especially to poetry, lived, during the Renaissance, Boiardo (1434-94), Ariosto (1474-1533), and Tasso (1544-95), among others. Their residence from 1385 onwards was the Castello (Plate 74) built by Bartolino Ploti da Novara.

75 The Cathedral with its elaborate Romanesque façade was built about 1135 by Wiligelmus and Nicolò: the upper arcades and the tympanum over the main doorway were added at the beginning of the fourteenth century.

76-80 RAVENNA, the capital of the Romagna, was once situated on the sea and was notable for its harbour, built by order of Augustus. From 404 onwards it was the seat of the Western Emperor, then of Odoacer, Theodoric and the Byzantine Exarch. The architectural monuments, built for the most part of brick, testify to the unique importance of the city at the time of the barbarian invasions.

76 The buildings called the "Calchi" near the Palace of Theodoric may well have been put up in the eighth century of the Byzantine Exarchate, and perhaps served as a barracks: it was long mistakenly pointed out as the palace of Theodoric.

77 Theodoric the Great, King of the Ostrogoths (493-526), who aspired to a grand synthesis of the Germanic, Romanesque and Byzantine cultures in his kingdom, had this unique sepulchral monument erected during his lifetime. The building is round, with a cruciform vault, and is roofed with a mighty monolith 36 feet in diameter and 10½ feet thick.

78 The Pineta (pinewoods) of Ravenna, now greatly reduced, afforded Rome and Venice timber for shipbuilding.

79 San Vitale, the most elaborate Byzantine structure in the West, was built at the beginning of the sixth century by Julianus Argentarius and consecrated in 547. Choir and apse are richly decorated in vitreous mosaic, with representations from the Old and New Testaments, and of the Emperor Justinian and his Empress Theodora: the mosaics probably date from shortly before the middle of the sixth century.

80 The Basilica of S. Apollinare in Classe, some 3 miles south of the city, near the former harbour of Classe, was also built by Julianus Argentarius and consecrated in 549. The wonderful mosaics (sixth to seventh centuries) show, in the middle of the apse vault, St Apollinaris, the companion of St Peter and founder of the see of Ravenna.

81-82 The APENNINES between Bologna and Florence, with ancient arterial roads linking northern and central Italy by way of various passes, among them the Passo della Futa (2,963 feet) and the Passo della Raticosa.

83 GENOA. A view of the harbour, the foremost in Italy, surrounded amphitheatre-wise by the city. The old capital of Liguria became Roman in 222 B.C. From the eleventh century it developed, in rivalry with Pisa and later with Venice, to become one of the leading sea-powers of the Mediterranean.

84 The fishing-village of PORTOFINO on the Riviera di Levante.

85 S. MARGHERITA LIGURE, a holiday resort and water-ing-place in the Riviera di Levante.

86 RAPALLO. The esplanade and the castle (thirteenth century) of this little town on the Riviera di Levante, well known as a venue for conferences.

87 Pinewoods on the Riviera di Levante, with a view towards Chiavari and the Bay of Sestri.

88–91 PISA, in Tuscany, lying at the mouth of the Arno, flourished as a maritime Republic in the tenth to thirteenth centuries, a rival of Genoa and Venice for the commerce of the Mediterranean. The city's fate was closely bound up with that of the house of Hohenstaufen; she served as Imperial seat of govern-ment for Italy. The existing Cathedral, Campanile and Baptistery were planned as portions only of a huge Forum, which was to have been worthy of an Imperial capital.

88 The Piazza dei Cavalieri was the centre of the mari-time city-state in the Middle Ages. The church of S. Stefano dei Cavalieri, designed by Vasari (1565–9), who also renovated the neighbouring Palazzo dei Cavalieri (1562), is, like it, a relic of the Medici domination. The Grand Duke Cosimo I, whose statue stands in the Piazza, had in 1561 founded the Order of Knights of St Stephen to combat piracy, and the palace and church were the seat of the Order.

89 The Campanile, the celebrated "Leaning Tower" in white marble, was in building from 1173 onwards and completed in 1360, in its present form; as originally planned, it was to have been appreciably higher, a pharos with a golden spire pointing to heaven. Since Galileo, a Pisan by birth, used the inclination of the tower (which was already manifest during its build-ing) for researches into the laws of gravity, this has become more pronounced. On the left is the Cathedral.

90 The Baptistery is the work of Diotisalvi, who began the building in 1152, Niccolò and Giovanni Pisano (second half of the thirteenth century) and various masters who completed it in the fourteenth century. In the background is the façade of the Cathedral, also in white marble, begun 1063, consecrated 1118 and finished in the twelfth to thirteenth centuries.

91 The Pulpit by Giovanni Pisano, restored to its original position in the Cathedral in 1926, with cer-tain replacements of lost parts. With its dramatically animated scenes from the life of Christ it forms a pendant to the equally famous pulpit by Niccolò Pisano, father of Giovanni, in the Baptistery (1260).

92–93 LUCCA, a free commune from 1119 onwards, came in the fourteenth century under various overlords, became a city-state in 1370 and retained her independ-ence almost uninterruptedly until 1805. The church of San Frediano (Plate 92) was built in 1112–47. The Lombardic campanile served, by its position close to the city wall, as a fortified tower. The Cathedral (Plate 93), an episcopal see already in the eighth century and several times rebuilt, received the upper part of its façade, by Giudetto da Como, in the year 1204. The Campanile was finished in the thirteenth century.

94–95 PISTOIA, the ancient *Pistoriae*, was during the Middle Ages a commune of Ghibelline sympathies, frequently in conflict with Lucca, Prato and Florence, and finally lost her independence to the latter. The Ospedale del Ceppo is a leper-hospital of the thirteenth to fourteenth centuries. At the beginning of the four-teenth century the Florentine administration had the portico built by the workshops of the della Robbia. Giovanni carried it out in 1514–25 with help from his pupils, and did the frieze in glazed terra-cotta with representations of the Works of Mercy.

96 PRATO, a noted centre of the textile, and especially of the wool industry from mediaeval times, was united to Florence in 1351. At the south-west angle of the Cathedral, a Romanesque basilica erected in the eighth to ninth centuries and altered in the fourteenth, is the "Pulpit of the Holy Girdle", finished in 1439, with a frieze of dancing putti by Donatello. From here the reliquary of the Holy Girdle is shown to the people.

97–105 FLORENCE, on the Arno in fertile Tuscany, an Etruscan foundation, was destroyed in 82 B.C. by Sulla, rebuilt as a colony by Julius Caesar in 59 B.C., became an espiscopal see about A.D. 300, and develop-ed from the eleventh century onwards as an in-dependent commune. In her commercial and political heyday in the thirteenth to fifteenth centuries (banking, textiles and commerce, guilds), literature and painting burgeoned in spite of party and family feuds, until in the reign of the rich Medici, Cosimo (d. 1464) and his grandson Lorenzo il Magnifico (d. 1492), the city achieved a cultural flowering comparable to that of Periclean Athens. In 1737 Florence came under the Habsburgs, and from 1865 till 1871 it was the capital of the new Kingdom of Italy.

97 View from the tower of the Signoria towards the Cathedral with its dome by Brunelleschi (1461) and Giotto's tower.

98 The Ponte Vecchio, the oldest of the city's bridges over the Arno, was rebuilt in 1345, after floods had destroyed the bridge first mentioned in 996. From the beginning the present bridge was provided with shops.

99 The Cathedral of Santa Maria del Fiore was begun on September 8th, 1296 by Arnolfo di Cambio on orders from the city; his instructions were to endow the building with "the finest and most sumptuous splendour" that human art could enlist. After Arnolfo's death in 1302 Francesco Talenti and Lapo Ghini carried on his work, to be followed after 1366 by various Boards of Works. Pope Eugene IV consecrated the building in 1436, but it was not finished till the addition of Brunelleschi's cupola in 1461. The present west front dates from the nineteenth century. The Campanile was begun by Giotto in 1334, and finished after his death by Andrea Pisano and Francesco Talenti in about 1359.

100 The Pitti Palace was built from 1458 onwards, to Brunelleschi's design for Luca Pitti, and extended by Ammannati between 1558 and 1570. From 1550 till 1859 it served as the residence of the Grand Duke of Tuscany, but is now a famous picture gallery. Says Burckhardt in his *Cicerone*, "This palace attains more nearly to the sublime than any other secular edifice in the world, including much larger buildings. Its situation on rising ground and its truly great dimensions enhance this effect, but in essence it depends upon the relationship of the forms, which recur with minor variations, to these dimensions. One asks oneself, who might be the world-despising man of power, who furnished with such means could banish everything merely pretty or pleasant?"

101 The courtyard of the Palazzo del Podestà or Bargello. Since 1859 it has served as a museum and contains the collections of Tuscan sculpture, medals, terra-cottas, etc., brought together in the Museo Nazionale, especially works of such great Renaissance masters as Donatello, della Robbia, Pollaiuolo and Verrocchio.

102 Piazza della Signoria. A view from the Loggia della Signoria or dei Lanzi (1376) of the façade of the Palazzo della Signoria or Palazzo Vecchio (1298-1314), the seat of the Florentine Republic, where in 1865-71 the Parliament of the new Kingdom of Italy met. In front of the palace is Michelangelo's David (1501-3), a copy of the great marble statue which stood here from 1504 till 1873 and is now in the Galleria dell'Accademia.

103 The Piazza and church of Sto Spirito. Begun in 1444 by Brunelleschi, it was not until 1479-81 that the church received the dome by Salvi d'Andrea; the Campanile by Baccio d'Agnolo was added from 1503-17 and 1568-71.

104 Sta Maria Novella (after 1350), known as Chiostro Verde on account of the dominating colour of the frescoes, now partly perished; one of the cloisters of the great Dominican monastery, which was the counterpart of Sta Croce, the headquarters of the Franciscans.

105 The Boboli Gardens, laid out by Tribolo in 1550, are, with their boscages and decorative statuary, the foremost example of the Florentine garden as it used to be cultivated even on the estates surrounding the city.

106-7 SAN GIMIGNANO. Situated on a Tuscan hill, 1,092 feet high. This town, which lost its political significance about the middle of the fourteenth century, and submitted to Florence, has preserved its mediaeval character particularly well. Of the tall family towers, characteristic of north Italian cities, by which the noble families sought to outdo one another, thirteen still remain; there used to be seventy-two here.

108-9 TUSCAN LANDSCAPES. A view from San Gimignano over the terraced hills (Plate 108), and a reach of the Arno between Florence and Arezzo (Plate 109).

110 AREZZO, once an important Etruscan centre, became a city-republic in 1098 and was finally defeated by her rival Florence in 1384. The Romanesque campanile of the church called S. Maria della Pieve, was finished in 1330.

111-12 SIENA, the *Sena Julia* of antiquity, independent from 1175 onwards, was the leading Ghibelline commune and Florence's chief rival among the cities of Tuscany. During the flowering of architecture, sculpture and painting in the thirteenth and fourteenth centuries, she became one of Italy's foremost art-centres.

111 The Palazzo Pubblico facing the roughly semicircular Piazza del Campo ranks as the finest Gothic palace in Tuscany. It was built in 1297-1310, in stone and (for the upper storeys) brick. The tower, 335 feet high, the Torre del Mangia, by Muccio and Francesco di Rinaldo, dates from 1338-48; the Cappella di Piazza with its open loggia was built in 1376 and enlarged in 1468.

112 The Cathedral was begun at the end of the twelfth century in the Romanesque style, but later, Gothic elements were incorporated. Its triple-gabled façade of marble is one of the finest creations of Giovanni Pisano, who built the lower part in 1284-99. Giovanni di Cecco finished the façade after 1376.

113 The central APENNINES, predominantly bare and showing characteristic erosion-patterns, form the watershed between Tuscany and the Romagna, or between Umbria and the Marches. The lowest crossing is the Passo di Montecoronaro (2,838 feet), which leads from the Tiber valley into the valley of the Savio, a river flowing eastwards towards the Adriatic.

114 UMBERTIDE, a little Umbrian town on the left bank of the Tiber.

115 Near SARSINA, in the valley of the Savio, on the eastern slopes of the Apennines in the Romagna.

116-17 RIMINI, the *Ariminum* of antiquity, was an Umbrian and subsequently a Celtic settlement; from 268 B.C. onwards it was a Roman colony, of particular importance due to its position at the end of the Flaminian Way (220 B.C.). The Arch of Augustus (Plate 116) was erected in 27 B.C. in honour of the Emperor and his road-building, at the point where the Via Flaminia from Rome joins the Via Emilia, running north. The Ponte d'Augusto (Plate 117), begun by Augustus and completed under Tiberius, crosses the river Marecchia.

118 ANCONA, the capital of the Marches, and one of the most important harbours on the Adriatic Coast, was founded about 390 B.C. by Syracusans and came into Roman possession in the third century B.C. The Arch of Trajan, the work of Apollodorus of Damascus, was erected in A.D. 115 to celebrate the completion of the natural harbour under Trajan's orders.

119 The town of LORETO, situated on the right bank of the river Musone not far from the Adriatic Coast, is famous for its pilgrimage-church. Beneath the dome is the "House of Mary" which, after the surrender of 1291, when Nazareth was overrun by the Mohammedans, is supposed to have been transported by angels on to the hill of Tersatto in Dalmatia, and in 1294 brought to Loreto. Benedict XV named the Madonna of Loreto as patroness of aviation. Among those who worked on the sanctuary of the Holy House were Giuliano da Maiano (1468), Giuliano da Sangallo and Bramante. Luigi Vanvitelli built the campanile in 1750-4: the vast Palazzo Apostolico was begun by Sansovino in 1510.

120 Between Cattolica in Emilia and Pesaro in the Marches, road and railway leave the immediate proximity of the Adriatic Coast and pass through hilly and intensively cultivated country.

121 FOSSOMBRONE, an episcopal see in the Marches, lies on the left bank of the river Metauro, on the old Via Flaminia.

122-4 URBINO, the home of Bramante and Raphael, came under the sway of the Count of Montefeltro in the fourteenth century, and was, under Federigo II (1444-82, Duke from 1474) and Guidobaldo (1472-1508), one of the most brilliant art-centres in Italy. Among those who worked at the ducal court were Luciano and Francesco Laurana, Leon Battista Alberti, Desiderio da Settignano, Piero della Francesca, Pisanello, Paolo Uccello, and

Melozzo da Forlì. The city stands on a height, with a prospect over the hilly landscape, and is dominated by the Ducal Palace (Plate 124), which was enlarged from 1465 onwards by Luciano Laurana; from him derives also the arrangement of the west front with its two slender round towers ". . . unique in Italy. In magnificence of conception, nobility of proportion and outline, Luciano here excels all his contemporaries and his work can at times hardly be distinguished from that of his pupil Bramante." (Burckhardt: *Cicerone*.)

125 On the BURANO, a small tributary of the Metauro in the Marches.

126 CANTIANO in the Marches, on the Via Flaminia.

127-8 PERUGIA, the ancient *Perusia*, one of the twelve cities in the Etruscan League, became Roman in 310 B.C. In the fourteenth and fifteenth centuries it was the most powerful State in Umbria, but as a result of internal discords it later came under the domination of the Popes. At the time of the Renaissance it was the centre of the Umbrian school of painting (Perugino and Pinturicchio). The city lies on a steep hill above the Tiber valley: the view from the highest point on the north side takes in the northern quarter (Plate 128) with S. Agostino and parts of the Etruscan fortifications. On the Piazza Quattro Novembre stands the Fontana Maggiore (Plate 127), built to a design by Fra Bevignate (1275-7). The reliefs are by Niccolò and Giovanni Pisano and were probably made in collaboration with Arnolfo di Cambio. In the background is the Palazzo Comunale or Palazzo dei Priori (1293-1443).

129 The Basilica of Sta Maria degli Angeli, in the plain below Assisi, was built in 1569 to the design of Galeazzo Alessi. Finished with help from Vignola in 1679 (it was faithfully rebuilt by L. Poletti after the earthquake of 1832), its precincts include the Porziuncola, the praying-chamber of St Francis of Assisi, his cell, his rose-garden and other places visited by the faithful in remembrance of the Poverello.

130-3 ASSISI, a little town on one of the foot-hills of Monte Subasio in Umbria, owes its renown to St Francis.

The son of a merchant, he was born here in 1182; in 1208 he founded the Franciscan Order of friars. In 1228, only two years after his death, he was canonized and the church over his grave grew into a national shrine and place of pilgrimage. Plate 131 shows the Franciscan monastery on its massive foundations. Plate 130 shows the Piazza by way of which the so-called Lower Church is entered; Plate 132, the west front of the Upper Church. The Basilica San Francesco was built between 1228 and 1253 and renovated in the following century. Both the crypt-like Lower Church and the Upper Church contain magnificent frescoes by Cimabue, Giotto, and the latter's pupils Simone Martini and Pietro Lorenzetti.

133 In the main square of the town stands the Temple of Minerva, dating from the time of Augustus, of which Goethe wrote: ". . . the first complete monument of antiquity that I ever saw; a modest temple, as was fitting for so small a town, and yet so perfect, so beautifully conceived, that it would show up anywhere".

134 Above one of the upper valleys of the Abruzzi rise the peaks of the Gran Sasso d'Italia, snow-capped even in summer, with the Corno Grande (9,560 feet), the highest peak of the Apennines.

135 The little town of ANTRODOCO lies on the river Verlino in the Abruzzi, near the junction of three gorges.

136-8 L'AQUILA, the capital of the Abruzzi, was founded in 1240 by the Emperor Frederick II. The massive Castle (Plate 136) was built in 1535 by Charles V. In the background is the Gran Sasso massif.

137 The white and red patterned façade of Sta Maria di Collemaggio. The church, begun in 1287, contains the grave of the hermit Pietro da Morrone, declared a saint in 1313. In August 1294, in this church, he had to take up his duty as Pope Celestine V, but the office ill suited his unworldly nature, and he resigned again after only five months.

138 The church of San Bernardino was built in 1472, over the grave of St Bernardino of Siena, a Franciscan renowned as a popular preacher, who died in Aquila

in 1444. In 1527 Cola d'Amatrice added the Renaissance-style façade.

139–40 LUGNANO IN TEVERINA and AMELIA, two little towns on the so-called Strada Amerina. Both are situated on hills above the Tiber valley, amid richly cultivated country in southern Umbria.

141 SPOLETO, the Roman *Spoletium*, the seat of a Lombard dukedom from 570 onwards, was destroyed in 1155 by Frederick Barbarossa and became part of the Papal States in the thirteenth century. The Ponte delle Torri, one of the most impressive of mediaeval bridges, received its present form in the fourteenth century. It is 755 feet long and its ten arches rise 260 feet above the river Ticino.

142–3 ORVIETO, an old Etruscan town, torn by intestine strife during the Middle Ages, and repeatedly at war with Siena, Viterbo, Perugia and Todi, became a Papal city in 1450. The mediaeval buildings and the Cathedral, a landmark for miles around, stand on a hill of volcanic tufa, which rises like an island amid famous vineyards, 656 feet above the broad valley of the Paglia, a tributary of the Tiber.

143 A view of the central portion of the Cathedral façade, which reaches to a height of over 170 feet. It was the work of Lorenzo Maitani (1310–1330), Andrea Orcagna (1354) and Andrea Pisano (1347), who was, among other things, also responsible for the Madonna in the tympanum of the central portal. The mosaic decoration was renewed in the nineteenth century. The interior of the basilica, with its massive columns, contains notable frescoes.

144–5 VITERBO, renowned as "the city of beautiful women and elegant fountains", became a free commune in the eleventh century, and was the hub of the territories which the Marchesa Matilda of Tuscany donated to the Church in 1115. It frequently served as a papal residence in the thirteenth century. The Via S. Pellegrino (Plate 144), has preserved its mediaeval aspect particularly well. The Palazzo Papale (Plate 145), was built in 1257–66 as a papal residence, and the loggia was added in 1267. Several papal elections were held there, among them the election of Gregory X, which took place after a vacancy of

thirty-three months, and gave rise to the regulations for conclaves which are still in force today.

146 View from Montefiascone on to the LAKE OF BOL-SENA. This is over 70 square miles in area, and is the largest lake of volcanic origin in Italy.

147 The little town of RONCIGLIONE lies on a hill of tufa above the Rio Vicano, which flows out of the Lago di Vico. Among the blackened mediaeval buildings of tufa can be seen the Romanesque campanile of Sta Maria della Providenza, and, to the left, the cupola of the Cathedral.

148 TARQUINIA, dominated by the white tower of its Citadel, lies on a hill 3 miles from the Tyrrhenian Coast, near the Etruscan city which was closely connected with the early history of Rome, and was destroyed by the Saracens in the eighth or ninth century. The mediaeval city arose from the Roman *Corgnetum* and was renamed in 1922. The Etruscan necropolis, which lies between ancient Tarquinii and the modern Tarquinia, is the most important yet brought to light.

149 The main square of GROSSETO, the capital of the Maremma, with the Cathedral on the left. It was built in 1190–1250, and rebuilt in 1294 by Sozzo di Rustichino. On the right can be seen the Palazzo della Provincia (nineteenth century), and in the foreground a memorial to the Grand Duke Leopold II of Tuscany, who had the Maremma drained to combat malaria.

150–63 ROME, the city of the seven hills on the Tiber in Latium, the legendary foundation of King Romulus, developed during the fifth century B.C. from a city-republic to the "caput mundi", the mistress of the ancient world. She received her most imposing buildings under Augustus and during the first two centuries of the Empire. After her decline and spoliation during the barbarian invasions she gradually became important as the capital of the Papal Territory, especially after Charlemagne had been crowned Emperor there in 800. Under the art-loving Popes of the Renaissance and the Baroque a new and splendid Rome arose. In 1870 the city was captured by the Italian national army and became the capital of the unified Kingdom of Italy (and after 1946, of the Republic).

150 The Aurelian Wall of the third century forms a girdle round ancient Rome 11 miles long. The most massive of the ancient, though frequently renovated gates, through which even now the visitor enters the city, is the Porta S. Sebastiano. It was built by Honorius in the fifth century as the Porta Appia and gives on to the Appian Way. Belisarius completed it in 536 and provided it with its two round towers.

151 The Forum Romanum, in the centre of the ancient city at the foot of the Capitoline Hill, was the focal point of the Roman community under the kings, the Republic and the emperors. The building of its temples, halls, triumphal arches and oratorical tribunes accompanied the rise of Rome to world power; when these were destroyed during the relentless war of the Middle Ages against paganism, their ruin was the symbolic ruin of the ancient world. It was not until the nineteenth century that the debris was cleared from what still remained.
The view, from the foot of the Capitoline Hill along the Via Sacra, shows in the distance the Colosseum, the Campanile of S. Francesco Romana and the Arch of Titus. In the left foreground can be seen the columns of the Temple of Saturn, dedicated in A.D. 498; behind, the Temple of Antoninus and Faustina (second century). Beyond the column stumps of the Basilica Julia, built by Julius Caesar, stand the three slender columns of the Temple of the Dioscuri (Castor and Pollux) and the small Temple of Vesta. On the extreme right is the Palatine Hill, the earliest residential quarter of Rome, on which the Caesars later built their palaces.

152 The Isola Tiberina, on which the church of S. Bartolommeo with its Romanesque campanile (extreme left) occupies the former site of the Temple of Aesculapius; and the oldest existing bridge of the city, the Ponte Fabricio, of 62 B.C.

153 The Janiculus (Monte Gianicolo) with its public grounds, formerly the gardens of the Palazzo Corsini, rises beyond and above the seven hills of ancient Rome.

154 The Castel Sant'Angelo and the Ponte Sant'Angelo. The bridge was built by Hadrian in A.D. 136. It leads to his Mausoleum (begun A.D. 135, finished A.D. 140 by Antoninus Pius). Legend has it that in 599, when Rome was suffering from a pestilence, an angel appeared to Pope Gregory the Great above Hadrian's Mausoleum; its present name derives from this occurrence. This virtual fortress, built of dark peperino, once served as citadel for the popes. Repeatedly besieged, partly destroyed, then rebuilt and enlarged, it rose above the various vicissitudes of the city to endure down the centuries.

155 On the Piazza di Spagna the Barcaccia Fountain plays; it was designed by Pietro Bernini, father of the renowned Gian Lorenzo, in the shape of a boat. Behind it are the Spanish Steps, built a century later (1721–5). These 137 steps lead to the French church of Trinità dei Monti, founded in 1495 by Charles VIII of France. At the foot of the steps, on the right, stands the house in which Keats died in 1821.

156 The Fontana dei Fiumi, the quadruple fountain on the Piazza Navona in front of Borromini's Baroque façade of Sant'Agnese in Agone, is one of Bernini's finest creations. Illustrated is one of the four colossal statues (executed by his pupils), representing the Ganges as a personification of Asia. The waters were first made to play in the Pope's presence in 1651.

157 The Fontana di Trevi, the most massive of all the city's fountains, takes up the whole south front of the Palazzo dei Duchi di Poli. Begun in 1732 by Nicolò Salvi as the result of a competition initiated by Clement XII, it was, after Salvi's death, completed by Giuseppe Pannini (1762) and adorned with statues by the most eminent Roman sculptors of the time. The central niche is occupied by the triumphant figure of Neptune in his shell-car.

158 The church of San Clemente was built before 385 in honour of St Peter's third successor. In 1108 Pope Paschal II had the upper church built upon the ruins of the lower basilica, destroyed in 1084. It is the purest example of an early Christian basilica, with choir-screens, crypt, high altar and bishop's throne. The mosaics on the arch and walls of the apse date from the first half of the twelfth century.

159 The Capitol, though the smallest of the seven hills of Rome, has nevertheless since ancient times been the political and religious centre of the city. After the

restoration of the Senate in 1143 it regained significance as the seat of the city's administration. In the seventeenth century it was remodelled to Michelangelo's design: the monumental approach by shallow steps leads to the Piazza del Campidoglio, flanked by the Senatorial Palace, the Capitoline Museum and the Palazzo dei Conservatori. At the head of the steps, on the balustrade are the colossal statues of the Dioscuri, of later Imperial date, discovered in the sixteenth century; and in the middle of the Piazza stands the bronze equestrian statue of the Emperor Marcus Aurelius.

On the left can be seen the austere façade of the church of Sta Maria d'Aracoeli (1250), built on the highest point of the Capitol, where, according to legend, the Sibyl of Tibur announced the birth of Christ to the Emperor Augustus· "Ecce ara primogeniti Dei." The steep approach of 124 marble steps was presented by the Roman people in 1348 as a thank-offering for having survived a pestilence.

160 San Giovanni in Laterano. As Cathedral church of the Bishop of Rome, "Head and Mother of all the churches of Rome and of the earth" it was, until the time of the emigration to Avignon (1309), the seat of the Popes; and here, from 312 onwards, several important Councils were held. Time and again partially destroyed by war, earthquake and fire, the Basilica is today largely the work of Borromini· the principal eastern façade, built of travertine, is by Alessandro Galilei (1732–6).

161–2 San Pietro in Vaticano is the sepulchral church of St Peter, and the largest building in Christendom. On the site of the venerable basilica built by Constantine, Pope Nicholas V began a new building, but in 1506 Julius II gave Bramante the commission for a different scheme. After Bramante's death in 1514, Raphael took over the direction of the building. In 1547 Michelangelo was appointed architect, and the audacious dome was finished in 1570 to his designs. Under Pope Urban VIII Carlo Maderna, a Ticinese, added a long nave east of the crossing and closed it with an elaborate façade. It was Maderna, also, who was responsible for the design of the two fountains in the Piazza, a brilliant conception by which the jets of water are brought into the general architectural scheme. The disposition of the Piazza with its colonnades

is the inspired work of Bernini, who is said to have conceived the layout as representing the open arms of an archangel, whose body is St Peter's. Plate 161 shows the earlier of the two fountains, built in 1613, and Plate 162 a view from the colonnades of the façade and dome of St Peter's.

163 Two of the best-preserved monuments of ancient Rome: the so-called Temple of Vesta (on the left), which cannot be dated with any certainty, is circular, with marble Corinthian columns of pure Greek character, possibly of the time of Augustus. The other building, erroneously designated the Temple of Fortuna Virilis, dates from about 100 B.C.

164 The Via Appia was the first of the great military roads built by the Romans to bear the name of a consul. It was laid out in 312 B.C. by the Censor Appius Claudius Caecus, and ran from Rome through the Campagna to Capua; later it was extended to Brindisi. Beyond the Porta San Sebastiano (Plate 150) both sides of the road are lined for miles with tombs and other buildings, among which are the most important of the Catacombs. It was on the Appian Way that the Apostle Peter, fleeing from Rome, met his Lord and was moved to return and suffer martyrdom.

165 PALESTRINA is the ancient *Praeneste*. Its large Temple of Fortune used to take up almost the whole area in mediaeval times. That great master of church music, Palestrina, was born in, and took his name from this little town.

166–7 TIVOLI, the *Tibur* of antiquity, lies on a spur of the Sabine Mountains, 771 feet above the Roman Campagna. It was one of the places to which Roman grandees used to repair to spend the summer in their villas. Cardinal Ippolito d'Este had the former Benedictine monastery converted into a country seat in 1550, and adorned its splendid garden with spacious water-terraces and fountains. Plate 166 shows a view from the terrace down the central avenue of the garden, lined with cypresses which are said to be the tallest in Italy; Plate 167 shows the "Water-Organ" (Fontana dell'Organo Idráulico).

168 A view of the peaceful Campagna from CASTEL GANDOLFO, the Pope's summer residence by the

Alban Lake (Lago Albano) in the Roman Campagna.

169 FRASCATI lies 1,056 feet above the Roman Campagna, on the slope of the volcanic Alban Hills. In Renaissance times it became the select summer resort of the Roman aristocracy, who had their villas here laid out with sumptuous gardens. The Villa Aldobrandini or Belvedere was built in 1598–1603 by Giacomo della Porta for Cardinal Pietro Aldobrandini, a nephew of Clement VIII. In 1943–4 Frascati, then German headquarters, suffered heavily in an Allied air attack.

170 ITRI owed her importance in ancient times to her situation on a pass through which ran the Via Appia. In the Middle Ages the castle was a key point on the road from Rome to Naples.

171 CASERTA was the Versailles of the Kings of Naples. Charles III of Bourbon had the Palazzo Reale built in 1752–74 to plans made by Luigi Vanvitelli. Towards the end of the Second World War the palace served as headquarters of the British-American Mediterranean forces, and the capitulation of the Germans in Italy was signed here on April 29th, 1945.

172 On the VOLTURNO near Capua. The river forms a strategically important line from the Apennines to the Tyrrhenian Sea. Garibaldi fought a battle here and in the Second World War the front ran from Gaeta to the upper Volturno and on to Castel di Sangro.

173 S. MARIA CAPUA VETERE was in Imperial times the largest city of southern Italy, and was later destroyed by the Saracens. The Amphitheatre, 558 feet long and 459 feet broad, was built by Augustus on the site of a famous gladiatorial school. The slave-revolt of Spartacus broke out here in 73 B.C.

174 TROIA in Capitanata (Apulia). Its twelfth-century Cathedral has one of the earliest bronze doors (1119, by Oderisius of Benevento) cast in Italy on Byzantine lines.

175 MONTESARCHIO, west of Benevento, has a Castle and is the ancient *Caudium* beside the Caudine Forks.

176–7 BENEVENTO in Campania, the Roman *Beneventum*, originally *Maluentum*, was the capital of the Samnites. From 571 till 1038 the city, situated at an important cross-roads, was the seat of a flourishing Lombard duchy. Before its walls Pyrrhus was defeated in 275 B.C., and in A.D. 1266 Manfred, the son of Frederick II. During the Second World War it suffered serious damage.

176 The Monastery of Santa Sofia, founded by a Lombard prince, has a Romanesque cloister (now a museum). For a long time it was the first learned establishment of Benevento: it shone so conspicuously in theological, Scholastic and grammatical studies in the ninth century, that the "philosophers of this city were famed throughout Italy" (Gregorovius).

177 The Arch of Trajan (Porta Aurea), built in A.D. 114, is the most elaborately ornamented Roman monument of its kind to survive. Its bas-reliefs depict scenes from the Emperor's life.

178–83 POMPEII, a flourishing Roman provincial town, suffered a severe earthquake in A.D. 63. It was partly rebuilt, but on August 24th, 79 it was buried in ashes by a fearful eruption of Vesuvius. The excavations, initiated in 1748, caused world-wide interest and served to re-awaken interest in the Antique. The plan of the city now exposed has proved one of the principal sources for our knowledge of everyday life in Roman times. The work of the archaeologists, which has been systematically carried out only since 1860, is even now not yet complete.

178 From the Porta di Ercolano, the western gate of the town, one of the ancient roads which are lined with numerous tombs (hence the name Via dei Sepolcri), leads in the direction of the Villa dei Misteri.

179 A view through the colonnade (dating from Samnite times) on the south side of the Forum, across the 466-feet-long square towards the Temple of Jupiter, with Vesuvius in the background.

180 On the west side of the Forum, behind the remains of the two-storeyed colonnade, is the (also two-storeyed) Basilica, once the centre of the city's commercial life.

181 The Temple of Apollo, with a peristyle of 48 columns, and with steps leading to the altar, goes back to the Samnite period. The original of the bronze statue of Apollo is now in the National Museum in Naples, and the one seen here is a copy.

182 The "House of the Faun" (Casa del Fauno), one of the most beautiful remaining dwelling-houses of antiquity, was named after the bronze figure of the dancing satyr (original now in the Naples Museum) which decorated the impluvium of the entrance-hall. The famous Alexander mosaic was also found in this house.

183 The House of Loreius Tiburtinus has important frescoes; the layout of the garden is particularly charming.

184-5 NAPLES, beautifully situated in its Bay, between Vesuvius and the Phlegraean Fields, is one of the most important ports of the Mediterranean and was for long the most populous city of Italy (today it comes third after Rome and Milan). Neapolis ("the new city") dates back to a Greek colony of the eighth century B.C. Under Rome, too, it remained until late Imperial times, the capital of Hellenic culture in Italy. It was held by the Normans in the eleventh and twelfth centuries. In the thirteenth century, under Frederick II, it came once more into its own, and became the cultural capital of southern Italy. After the execution of Conrad by Charles of Anjou, in 1268, Naples served as capital of the Kingdom of the Two Sicilies under the Angevins who were later supplanted by Aragonese, the Habsburgs and the Bourbons; in 1860 Garibaldi brought about its unification with the Italian national State.

184 The Castel Nuovo, built under Charles I of Anjou in 1279-82, served the Angevin, Aragonese and Spanish Viceroys as their official residence. The magnificent Renaissance triumphal arch between the two fortified towers was built in 1453-67, in honour of Alfonso I of Aragon, probably to the design of Francesco Laurana and with the assistance of various sculptors.

185 View from the hill opposite Posilipo towards Naples and Vesuvius. In the middle distance is the island with the Castel dell'Ovo; the trees on the left mark the grounds of the Villa Nazionale, with the Zoological Station founded by Andreas Dohrn in 1872, and the Aquarium.

186 A view from the coast near Sorrento to the island of CAPRI, at the entrance to the Bay of Naples. On account of its natural beauty and its mild climate Capri was used already by Augustus and Tiberius as a holiday resort.

187 SORRENTO, the ancient Surrentum, birthplace of Torquato Tasso, lies, surrounded by walnut-trees, orange- and lemon-groves and vineyards, on the Sorrentine Peninsula overlooking the Bay of Naples.

188-9 POSITANO is a little harbour-town on the precipitous Amalfi Coast, surrounded by olive-groves. Many of the cubical houses have bowl-shaped domes which give it an Oriental charm.

190 AMALFI, the oldest Italian maritime Republic, reached her greatest power after the defeat of the Saracen invasions in about A.D. 1000. As a result of her defeats by Pisa in 1135 and 1137 she fell out of competition with Genoa and Pisa as a trading-city; but her maritime code, as embodied in the Tavole Amalfitane, was valid over the entire Mediterranean until 1570.

191-2 Minori and the Amalfi Coast on the Gulf of Salerno.

193 ATRANI with the church of the Maddalena, on the Amalfi Coast.

194 A view from the Amalfi Coast with one of its old castles, across the GULF OF SALERNO. In the distance, the town of Salerno, the seat of a principality which was for a time Lombard and later Norman. The Allied landing in the Gulf of Salerno (September 8th, 1943) was one of the decisive events in the Italian campaign of 1943-4.

195-7 PAESTUM, the Greek Poseidonia, in the south of the Gulf of Salerno, was founded by the Sybarites in the sixth century B.C. and was a flourishing Greek colony in the sixth and fifth centuries. It was captured in the fourth century by the Lucanians, and in 273 B.C. by the Romans; in late Imperial times it became depopulated owing to malaria. Its three Doric temples are among the finest and best preserved of all Greek buildings.

195 In the foreground the so-called Temple of Poseidon (more probably the Temple of Hera) of the fifth century: a massive peripteral temple, 197 feet by 97 feet, built of travertine. In the background is the so-called Basilica, of the sixth century, the oldest of the Paestum temples.

196 The Temple of Ceres, dating from the end of the sixth century.

197 The so-called Basilica, with a view towards the mountains of the southern Apennines which rise beyond the coastal plain.

198 West of the town of LUCERA, in a commanding situation in Capitanata, stands the castle built by Frederick II. The Hohenstaufen emperor had settled more than 20,000 Saracens in "Lucera Saracenorum", and with their help had erected one of the strongest fortresses in his dominions.

199 The view from the height of Troia towards Lucera over CAPITANATA in Apulia, with the great plain of the Tavoliere.

200 CASTEL DEL MONTE, visible from far away, 1,900 feet up on a hill of the Murge, was built about 1240 by Frederick II as a grand memorial to this unique sovereign personage. "The forms are of a classic simplicity and purity", wrote Gregorovius, which compels admiration and sets a high standard for Hohenstaufen architecture in Italy. "The heavy fortress-like aspect is perfectly transcended; the Gothic itself is clarified by the antique feeling for form.... All is harmoniously arranged, carried out according to a single principle, light and airy, elegant yet of great solidity."

201 Under Byzantine and, later, Norman rule during the Crusades and especially under Frederick II, TRANI was one of the most important harbours on the Adriatic. The Romanesque cathedral was begun in 1094 and finished in the thirteenth century, together with its 213-foot campanile.

202 MOLFETTA, a fishing and trading harbour on the Adriatic, with its Byzantine Duomo Vecchio (thirteenth century).

203-4 BARI, the capital of Apulia and second only to Naples as a commercial centre of southern Italy, was an important harbour even in antiquity. It was a Saracen stronghold in the ninth century. The Romanesque basilica of S. Nicola (on the right in Plate 203) was begun in 1087, to contain the bones of St Nicholas, Bishop of Myra: the entry into the town of the popular saint and patron of seafarers is celebrated here with a great festival on May 8th. On the far side of the square is the church of S. Gregorio (eleventh century). The citadel (Plate 204) is one of the strongholds which Frederick II built for himself in Apulia (1233-40); the surrounding wall is early sixteenth century.

205 BRINDISI, the Roman *Brundisium*, was important both as a harbour and as the termination of the Via Appia. Later, it belonged in turn to Byzantium and to the Saracens, and after the opening of the Suez Canal flourished again as a harbour and port of embarkation. The Romanesque church of San Giovanni al Sepolcro, a round church built by the Templars in the twelfth century, and later taken over by the Knights of the Holy Sepulchre, is now used as the Museo Civico.

206-9 MURGIA DEI TRULLI, with Alberobello (Plate 208) and Locorotondo (Plate 209) is the district of Apulia which takes its name from the type of building found there in considerable numbers—the "Trulli". "Thousands of years before the birth of Christ the aboriginal Messapians were building dome-shaped buildings of rude stone—tombs, shrines and dwellings. Not a single legend survives to tell of the people who first built these monuments, or of their beliefs, but the shape of their houses has remained unaltered. There are in the interior whole villages in which all the houses and the churches themselves are Trulli. Each room has its dome, and an inn in Alberobello has 23 of them, which rise beside and above one another like the huts of central Asia." (Hector G. Precori.) The Trulli also serve sometimes, as in Plate 207, the purpose of little grape-houses in the vineyards. Plate 206 shows the view from Martina Franca towards Locorotondo.

210-11 TARANTO, an Italian naval base, was founded in 708 B.C. by the Spartans and was one of the most successful Greek colonies in southern Italy. It became Roman in 272 B.C. and belonged to Byzantium until well into the Middle Ages. The Citadel (Plate 210), built in 1480 by Ferdinand of Aragon, and enlarged in 1577, dominates the channel which connects the "Mare Grande", the open sea, with the "Mare Piccolo", the large basin and natural harbour. Plate 211 shows the fishing-harbour.

212–14 From LAGONEGRO (Plate 212), 2,185 feet up on the Monte del Papa of the Lucanian Apennines, the road leads through mountain landscape with volcanic cones, out of Basilicata to Morano Calabro (Plate 214), the ancient *Muranum*, 1,800 feet up on Monte Pollino (7,375 feet).

215–16 TAORMINA, in Sicily, the Greek *Tauromenion*, lies in a uniquely beautiful situation 670 feet up on Monte Tauro above the Ionian Sea. Plate 215 shows the view of the coast, looking towards the Gulf of Messina. Plate 216, the theatre, Greek but rebuilt by the Romans; beyond the stage the spectators used to be able to see the snow-covered cone of Etna (10,758 feet).

217–19 SYRACUSE in Sicily has an excellent natural double harbour formed by its mainland and the little island of Ortygia. It was founded in 735 B.C. by Corinthians, and developed into one of the most brilliant cities of Greek antiquity, very much larger than the present provincial capital. Its decline began with its conquest by Rome in 212 B.C. The great theatre (Plate 217) was probably built in the fifth century under Hiero and later enlarged: it is 440 feet in diameter. The spectators enjoyed a view over the town and harbour.

218 In the so-called Latomie, underground quarries, later largely collapsed through earthquakes, the material for the city's buildings was obtained. In the Latomia del Paradiso is the Grotta dei Cordari, a large cave supported by natural pillars, which took its name from the rope-makers who used to work here.

219 The Cathedral, built in the seventh century and incorporating the remains of a Temple of Minerva, was altered in 1693 and was given its Baroque façade by P. Picherale in 1728–57.

220 SELINUS (*Selinunte*), a Doric foundation of the seventh century B.C., was the westernmost of the Greek colonies in Sicily and flourished till it was first sacked by the Carthaginians in 409 B.C. The temple

illustrated is the oldest of the five in the city and was dedicated either to Apollo or to Heracles.

221 In the sixth and fifth centuries B.C., AGRIGENTUM, then known as *Akragas*, was one of the most prosperous cities of the Hellenic world, and counted Pindar and Aeschylus among its inhabitants. Its importance declined after its subjugation in 406 B.C. by Carthage and the ensuing rivalry between her and Rome. The Temple of Concord, built of shelly limestone weathered to a reddish colour, dates from the fifth century B.C. and owes its good state of preservation to the fact that in the sixth century it was converted into a church.

222 PALERMO (see also Plate 224). One of the Sicilian peasants' carts, which are gaily painted with scenes from Ariosto and other representations.

223 At MONREALE, near Palermo, the Norman King William II founded a Benedictine abbey in 1174 and had the Cathedral built nearby (1175–89). The basilica has three aisles, and its choir has kept the form of a Byzantine church. The mosaics, finished in 1182, cover the entire interior with brilliant and festive decoration: the Christos Pantokrator is represented above the enthroned Virgin in the semi-dome of the apse.

224 PALERMO, the capital of Sicily, was a Phoenician foundation (*Panormos*), and was successively Roman (253 B.C.), Saracenic (A.D. 831) and Norman (A.D. 1072). Frederick II made it the seat of a brilliant court in the first half of the thirteenth century. Here flourished the Sicilian school of poets, and Western culture was exposed to the influence of the art and science of the Arab world. The Cathedral, containing the tombs of Frederick II and other rulers, is one of the masterpieces of Norman architecture. It was founded in 1185 in honour of the Assumption. The southern entrance is through a portico.

225 SEGESTA (the Greek *Egesta*) was a city of the Elymi, who were continually at war with the Greek colonies, although they assimilated Greek culture. According to legend it was founded by Trojan refugees on the present Monte Barbaro, by the warm springs of Skamandros (Fiume Gaggera). It was destroyed in Saracen times. The unfinished temple dates from the second half of the fifth century B.C.

INDEX